WORLD CLUB

3

STUDENTS' BOOK

Longman

Michael Harris   David Mower

Summary of course content

Students' Book

Module 0: Learning to Learn page 4

Finding your way around the book
Using English in the classroom and outside school
Tackling a reading text and dealing with new words
Tackling a listening exercise
Writing an e-mail letter, editing and thinking about grammar

Module 1: Cities page 9

READING:	a tourist guide; a newspaper article; a brochure
LISTENING:	a radio quiz; people in a London tourist office; teenagers talking; a song
SPEAKING:	cities; travelling in cities
WRITING:	description of a city; plans for the weekend; a tourist brochure
GRAMMAR:	questions; plans, intentions and arrangements Test Yourself
VOCABULARY:	cities; adjectives; phrasal verbs
PRONUNCIATION:	intonation in questions and answers; word stress

Module 2: Yesterday page 23

READING:	a biography; a legend; extracts from history books
LISTENING:	people in history and legend; an interview; a quiz
SPEAKING:	famous people in history; your life
WRITING:	a list of teenage rights; a biography
GRAMMAR:	the past simple (regular and irregular verbs); *used to*; Test Yourself
VOCABULARY:	people in history and legend; adjectives; wordbuilding; sequence words; jobs
PRONUNCIATION:	contractions; the letter 'i'

Module 3: Nature page 37

READING:	magazine articles; a leaflet; a letter to a newspaper
LISTENING:	a survey; a radio interview; a wildlife quiz
SPEAKING:	wild animals; 'green' issues; a debate
WRITING:	descriptions of animals; a list of 'green' suggestions; an ecological project
GRAMMAR:	comparative and superlative adjectives; conditional (type 1); Test Yourself
VOCABULARY:	seasons; animals, their habitats and characteristics; ecology; wordbuilding
PRONUNCIATION:	stress on key words; the letter 'o'

Activity Book

Module 0: Learning to Learn page 2

Personal information
Classroom language
Self-assessment
Grammar review

Module 1: Cities page 7

READING:	city guides; a teenager; Time to Read - *A different way of life*
LISTENING:	a radio programme
GRAMMAR:	common mistakes; questions; prepositions; plans, intentions and arrangements Test Yourself
VOCABULARY:	cities, adjectives to describe cities, adverbs of frequency, punctuation - capital letters
PRONUNCIATION:	word stress

Module 2: Yesterday page 16

READING:	extracts from history books; biographies; Time to Read - *Communications*
LISTENING:	facts about ancient China
GRAMMAR:	the past simple; *used to*; personal pronouns; adjectives; Test Yourself
VOCABULARY:	jobs; weapons; transport; adjectives to describe people; punctuation - apostrophes

Module 3: Nature page 25

READING:	a magazine article; Time to Read - *Cleaner fuel*
LISTENING:	an interview; a class debate
WRITING:	description of an animal
GRAMMAR:	comparative and superlative adjectives; question words; *should* for advice; conditional (type 1); future with *will*, Test Yourself
VOCABULARY:	animals and adjectives to describe them; punctuation - addresses

Students' Book

Module 4: Fantasy page 51

READING:	a magazine article; a diary; two strange stories
LISTENING:	dialogues; descriptions; stories
SPEAKING:	fantastic things; films and going to the cinema; telling stories
WRITING:	diary plans; story notes; the ending to a story
GRAMMAR:	the past simple and present perfect contrasted; the past continuous; Test Yourself
VOCABULARY:	fantasy and the supernatural; films and cinema; sequence words; adjectives; opposites
PRONUNCIATION:	the letter 'e'

Module 5: Sport page 65

READING:	a sports questionnaire; a magazine article; a TV guide; a student composition
LISTENING:	teenagers talking; an interview; TV commentaries
SPEAKING:	sports; famous sports people; your favourite sport
WRITING:	a school magazine article
GRAMMAR:	conditional (type 2); question tags; Test Yourself
VOCABULARY:	sports; adverbs of manner; sports equipment
PRONUNCIATION:	contractions; intonaton to express uncertainty; the letter 'a'

Module 6: Space page 79

READING:	an extract from a science book; a student composition; magazine articles
LISTENING:	a radio interview; a radio programme; a song
SPEAKING:	space travel; predictions for the future
WRITING:	predictions; notes; a horoscope
GRAMMAR:	predictions - *will, won't, may, might*; present simple passive; Test Yourself
VOCABULARY:	solar system; space travel; science-fiction; horoscopes; nouns; wordbuilding
PRONUNCIATION:	consonant clusters

Pairwork Activities	page 93
Reading Club 1–6	page 95
Mini-dictionary	page 98
End-of-year Self-Assessment	page 111
Irregular verb list	page 112
Phonetic Chart	page 112

Activity Book

Module 4: Fantasy page 34

READING:	maze reading; Time to Read - *A friendly dog*
LISTENING:	descriptions
GRAMMAR:	the present perfect and past simple contrasted; past and present continuous; Test Yourself
VOCABULARY:	fantasy and the supernatural; cinema; phrasal verbs; sequence words; adjectives to describe monsters; punctuation - sentences

Module 5: Sport page 43

READING:	a magazine article; a student composition, Time to Read - *The theory of sleep*
LISTENING:	unusual sports; a commentary
GRAMMAR:	conditional (type 2); quantity words; prepositions of time; question tags; modal verbs; Test Yourself
VOCABULARY:	TV programmes; sport; punctuation - apostrophes

Module 6: Space page 50

READING:	Time to read - *The future of the moon*
LISTENING:	a talking computer; the mystery of the Dogons; an astrologer
WRITING:	the future; space travel
GRAMMAR:	making plans and predictions; opinions; *how* questions; the passive; *there is/are*; Test Yourself
VOCABULARY:	space; wordbuilding; signs of the zodiac; punctuation - commas in lists

Maze story	page 57
Grammar file	page 60
Test Yourself - Answer Key	page 64

LEARNING

A Starting Off

a

Match the titles of the modules in this book with the pictures.

- Fantasy
- Nature
- Sport
- Cities
- Space
- Yesterday

Example: 1 = sport

b

Answer these questions about this book.

Example: 1 = six modules

1 How many modules are there?
2 How many lessons are there in every module?
3 What is in the *Module Check* section at the end of every module?
4 What page is the lesson *Champions* on?
5 What is the Language Focus in Lesson 1 about?
6 What is the name of the actress in the text on page 6?

c

In pairs, ask and answer more questions about the book.

Example: What famous sports stars are in the photos in Lesson 26?

d

MY LIFE GAME

Think of five sentences about your life, four true and one false.

Example: I can play the piano. I have got a dog called Eric. My favourite colour is blue. My sister is a doctor. I like photography.

In pairs, say your sentences to your partner. See if he/she can guess the false one!

B Speaking

a LEARN TO LEARN

In pairs, use the questionnaire to interview your partner.

1 Do you try to speak English in class?
   a usually **b** never **c** sometimes

2 When the teacher says something that you don't understand, what do you do?
   a ask the teacher to repeat in your language
   b say nothing
   c ask another student
   d ask the teacher to repeat in English

3 Do you ever feel nervous when you are speaking English?
   a no, never
   b only when I speak in front of the class
   c when I speak in groups

4 When you are speaking English and you don't know a word, what do you do?
   a stop speaking
   b try to say it using other words or use your hands and body
   c say the word in your language

5 When you make a mistake, what do you do?
   a continue speaking if people understand
   b stop speaking completely
   c if people don't understand, use different words

b

Listen to a teacher replying to eight questions from students. What do you think the questions were? Write them down.

Example: 1 How do you spell *dictionary?*
Listen again and check your answers.

c KEYWORDS

In pairs, use the questions from exercise B to test your partner about the words below.

Example: A: How do you spell cupboard?

B: C ~ U ~ P ~ B ~ O ~ A ~ R ~ D

> cupboard   dictionary
> pencil   bag   desk   glue
> wastepaper basket
> scissors   notebook   ruler
> blackboard   homework
> pencil sharpener   classroom

d KEYWORDS   LEARN TO LEARN

Where do *you* hear or see English outside your class? Tell the class.

Example: I sometimes hear foreign tourists speaking English in my town.

> foreign tourists   pop songs
> films at the cinema   videos
> television   letters   books
> magazines   comics   radio
> advertising   instructions
> names of products

Reading

a

In pairs, find out your partner's favourite film stars, sports stars and singers.

b

Before reading, in pairs, do the following:

- Look at the picture and title and guess what the photo is about.
- Guess where it is from (magazine/book).
- List what you know about the topic.

c

Now read the text quickly and find this information about Juliette Binoche.

nationality / date of birth / first big film / number of films / most successful role

Do not try to understand every word!

d

Read the text again and answer these questions.

1 Where did she start acting?
2 In which films did she have problems? Why?

FRENCH STAR IN THE ENGLISH PATIENT

Juliette Binoche became a world famous star for her role as Hanna, a French Canadian nurse, in the incredibly successful film *The English Patient*. In March 1997 she also became one of the first French actresses to win an Oscar.

Juliette was born in 1964 in Paris. When she was four her parents divorced and sent Juliette to a boarding school. She hated the school but she started acting there. "You had to make a private life for yourself, so you did it by being someone else, play acting."

When Juliette was eighteen she went to the National School of Dramatic Art in Paris. Her first big film was in 1984 with director Jean Luc Godard. Since then she has made over twenty films with French, British and Polish directors. She is also a successful model for perfumes.

When she started acting in English films Juliette had a few language problems, but she has worked hard on her English and it is now excellent. One thing is certain about Juliette Binoche, her future career will be interesting to watch!

e

List two examples of the following:

- Important words that you guessed the meaning of.
- Important words that you looked up in the mini-dictionary.
- Words that you ignored because they were not important.

f

Organise your vocabulary book, by topic or alphabetically. Write down important new words from this lesson. Include this information:

career - *n.* (noun) = a person's working life

Example: Juliette Binoche's career will be interesting to watch.

D Listening

a

In pairs, which of these statements about listening in *your* language do you agree with? Is it the same or different in English?

1 Some people are more difficult to understand than others.
2 It is easier to understand someone when you can see them speaking.
3 It is easier to understand tapes when you know something about the topic or situation.
4 Often you only try to understand part of what you hear (e.g.: watching the news on TV)
5 You need to understand every word when you listen to people.

b

It is useful to guess what you are going to hear *before* you listen. Do the following:

1 Look at the two photos. Guess how old the people are and where they are from.
2 Look at the table on the right and see what they are going to talk about.

Listen to the tape and find out if your predictions were right.

c

Copy the table, listen again and complete it for Maureen and Winston.

	MAUREEN	WINSTON	YOUR PARTNER
GETS UP		6.30	
FINISHES SCHOOL			
AFTER SCHOOL	homework/ reading		
WEEKENDS		swimming / playing cricket	

d

In pairs, find out about your partner's life and complete the table.

Example: What time do you get up?

e

Write down important new words from this lesson in your vocabulary book.

E Writing

a

Read the e-mail letter below and find out which information is mentioned.

age / family / holiday plans / favourite school subjects / teachers / likes and dislikes / hobbies

b

Read the letter again and correct the mistakes.

Example:
1 work = works

c

Find examples of these tenses in the corrected letter.

- Present simple (e.g.: I **live** in London.)
- Present continuous (e.g.: I **am studying** now.)
- Future with *going to* (e.g.: I **am going to** work hard this year.)
- Past simple (e.g.: I **went** to Ireland last year.)

Which tense do you have most problems with?

d

Write an e-mail letter about yourself to Tjeerd.

- Use the list in exercise A to **write notes** about yourself.
E.g.: family ~ parents, three brothers.
  - **Write** your message then **check it** for mistakes.
  - **Write a final version** (do not put your name).

e

In groups, mix the messages up. Then read them out and guess who they are from!

Date: 22/04/1999 18:46
To: <garcia@online.ve>
From: <greidanus@network.nl>

I am your new penfriend from Holland. I am fifteen years old and I have got one brother and one sister. My brother (1) work in a computer company in our town. My sister (2) start university at Leyden last year and she (3) is not live at home at the moment.

I am still at school but I (4) wants to study languages at university. This summer I (5) going to study Spanish in Salamanca. My favourite hobby in the winter is making model ships and in the summer I go sailing. What is Venezuela like? Write to me soon and tell me about yourself!

Best wishes,   Tjeerd

8

MODULE 1

CITIES

Lead-in

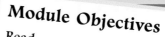

Module Objectives
In this module you will ...

Read a tourist guide, a newspaper article and a brochure.
Talk about city life, your free time activities and do a tourist role-play.
Listen to teenagers talking, a radio quiz and a rock 'n' roll song
Practise asking questions and expressing plans, intentions and arrangements.

Your **final tasks** will be to **write** a tourist brochure and do a **survey**.

a **LEARN TO LEARN** **KEYWORDS**

Look at the Keywords box. Decide if the words refer to positive or negative things about cities. Use the mini-dictionary in the back of the book.

Example: shops(+), traffic jams(-)

> shops   traffic jams   cinemas   restaurants
> pollution   discos   noise   museums
> parks   homeless people   top sports teams
> litter   crime

b

Look at the photos. In pairs, one student talks about the advantages of cities, the other talks about the disadvantages. The words in the box will help you.

Example: A: There are lots of big shops in cities.
B: Okay, but at night the streets are dangerous.

c **LEARN TO LEARN**

Now write new words in your vocabulary book.

9

1 City Quiz

A

Match the photos with these cities.

San Francisco / Istanbul / Seville / Venice /
Rio de Janeiro

B 🔑 KEYWORDS

Match the words with the definitions.

> air pollution   island   bridge   underground
> square   continent

1 an open area in a city surrounded by
   buildings
2 air made dirty by factories and cars
3 one of the large areas of land in the world
4 a train system below a city
5 a piece of land surrounded by water
6 a structure to carry a road or railway over
   a river or road

C 📼

**Is this information true or false? Listen to the
quiz and check your answers.**

1 Most people in the world live in cities.
2 Mexico City has a big air pollution problem.
3 There are over 100 islands in Venice.
4 The Golden Gate Bridge is in New York.
5 Rio de Janeiro is the capital of Brazil.
6 Istanbul is in two continents.
7 The 'Expo' world fair was in Seville in 1994.

Language Focus: Questions

D

Listen to the quiz again. Copy and complete the questions in the box with these words.

How many / Does / Where / Which / Do / What / When

1 ...	most people in the world live in cities?
2 ...	Mexico City have an air pollution problem?
3 ...	islands are there in Venice?
4 ...	is the Golden Gate Bridge?
5 ...	is the capital of Brazil?
6 ...	city is in two continents?
7 ...	was the 'Expo' world fair in Seville?

Did you know?

Urungi, in China, is the furthest city from the sea – about 2,250km away!

E

Write questions using the cues. Then match them with the answers.

Example: **1** What is the capital of Germany?
      b Berlin.

1 ... the capital of Germany?
2 ... the lost city of Machu Picchu?
3 ... Moscow have an underground?
4 ... the original name of New York?
5 ... people live in Mexico City?
6 ... the longest underground?
7 ... most people travel by car in Beijing?
8 ... city of York founded?

a London - it has got 400km of track!
b Berlin
c No. Most travel by bicycle.
d In 71 AD
e Near Cuzco
f Yes, a very good one.
g Over 15 million
h New Amsterdam

PRONUNCIATION

F

Listen to the first four questions from exercise D. Does the intonation go up or down?

Example: Do most people in the world live in cities?

G

YOUR CITY QUIZ

In pairs, take turns to ask questions. Student A looks at number 1 on page 93 and Student B looks at number 1 on page 94. Then, make up some more questions with your partner to ask another pair.

2 Great Cities

Cairo

1 Cairo, on the impressive River Nile, is a fascinating city of great contrasts. Arabs founded the city in 641, and it has been the centre of Egypt for centuries. Now it is the largest city in Africa, a busy city full of character, with an exciting mixture of ancient and modern.

Places to see: In the city there are many magnificent mosques and you can visit the Egyptian Museum to see the wonderful treasures of Tutankhamen. Outside Cairo are the Sphinx and the monumental pyramids, one of the Seven Wonders of the World.

On the menu: Try specialities like kebabs. Finish off your meal in style with some delicious sweet coffee.

Paris

2 Paris, which became capital of France in the sixth century, is at the heart of French history and civilisation. Paris is famous for food, cosmetics, art and fashion. Many people think Paris is the most romantic city in the world.

Places to see: There are many wonderful places to visit and things to do. See the superb buildings in the Place Vendôme. Take a boat trip on the Seine and see the historic bridges. Relax in one of the smart cafés in the Champs-Élysées.

On the menu: Paris is the home of French cuisine. On a cold day start with some *soupe à l'oignon* (onion soup). *Moules marinières* (mussels in cream sauce) makes a tasty main course. Try some mouth-watering profiteroles for dessert.

London

3 London has been the capital of England since Roman times. It is the financial and commercial centre of Britain, full of historic buildings and modern amenities. London is now an international city, home to cultures from around the world.

Places to see: Of course, go to famous London landmarks like Big Ben and the Tower of London, but don't forget the museums. The Victoria and Albert Museum is magnificent. In the evening, treat yourself to an exciting musical at one of London's excellent theatres.

On the menu: Fifty years ago, London had a reputation for poor quality food. Not any more. You can now get wonderful meals. For a main course, try traditional favourites like steak and kidney pie.

A
CITY GAME

In groups, one student names a city. Then, take turns to say cities beginning with the same letter.

Example: Casablanca, Cairo, Caracas ...

B
Which city would you like to visit? Tell the class.

Example: I'd like to visit New York.

C

Read the brochure. Are these sentences true or false?

1 Cairo is near a river.
2 Cairo is the largest city in Africa.
3 You can see the Sphinx in the Egyptian Museum.
4 Paris has been the capital of France for more than 1000 years.
5 Paris is a good place to buy clothes.
6 The Seine is the name of a bridge.
7 There are many different cultures in London now.
8 The Tower of London is a famous museum.
9 London has always been famous for good food.

D

Read the text again. Copy and complete this table with adjectives.

CITIES	FOOD	BUILDINGS
fascinating	delicious	magnificent

Underline the adjectives that are similar in *your* language.

E

Use the mini-dictionary at the back of this book to check the meanings and write new words in your vocabulary book. Do all the similar words have the same meanings in your language?

F

Decide if the sentences say positive, negative or neutral things about the cities.

Example: London is a dirty city. (-)
You can get delicious food in Paris. (+)
Cairo is in Africa. (+ -)

1 London is the capital of England.
2 Restaurants in Paris are expensive.
3 The Egyptian Museum is near the River Nile.
4 London has excellent theatres.
5 Taxis are difficult to find in Cairo.
6 Traffic is slow in London.
7 Cairo is an exciting mixture of ancient and modern.
8 Nine million people live in Paris.
9 There are lots of things to do in Paris.

G

What's the name of this city?

It's in the USA. It can be very dangerous. The air pollution from all the cars is very bad. Lots of film stars live there. It has got a Spanish name and more people speak Spanish there than English!

Now choose a city in your own country and write a similar description. Don't put the name!

H

Read your description to the class. The first one to guess the city wins.

3 Getting Around

A LEARN TO LEARN

What do you read in your own language? Which types of text do you read in English? Grade them like this:

✪✪✪ very difficult   ✪✪ ok   ✪ easy

- magazine articles
- brochures
- letters
- books (fiction)
- notices
- postcards
- books (non-fiction)
- newspapers

B

What type of text is the text below? Match the photos with the paragraphs.

Example: A = 3

GLOBAL TRAFFIC JAM

1 How long does it take you to get to school in the mornings? In some big cities it can take ages to go anywhere and millions of people spend hours sitting in traffic jams. For example, in Lima in Peru, the traffic is so bad during the rush hour that it is quicker to walk than to go by bus or car.

❖❖❖

POLLUTION DANGER

2 The problem with walking to school is that you have to breathe, and in many cities the air is not exactly clean. In some cities the pollution caused by cars is so dangerous that people wear masks in the street.

❖❖❖

NO CARS

3 There are very few cities with no cars. Venice is one of these and people get around on foot or by boat, by water buses or water taxis. It is more expensive to go by gondola and not very fast, but much more romantic!

PUBLIC TRANSPORT

4 In many places public transport also gets very crowded in rush hours. In Tokyo there are special workers to push people into the underground trains. But if you go by underground you can avoid traffic jams and public transport causes less pollution.

ON YOUR BIKE!

5 Perhaps the best way of getting around is by getting on your bike. It can be more dangerous but a lot of cities have special bicycle lanes. Going by bike does not cause any pollution and it is good exercise for you!

C

Read the text again. Copy and complete the table.

TRANSPORT	ADVANTAGES	DISADVANTAGES
Car	–	*traffic jams / pollution*
Underground		
Gondola		
Bicycle		

D

In groups, find out about other people's journey to school.

Example: A: How do you get to school?   B: On foot.
A: How long does it take you?   B: Twenty minutes.

Report the results of your group.

Example: Two people come by car and two by bus.
The average time it takes is fifteen minutes.

E

Complete this dialogue at a London tourist office.

A: Excuse me?
B: I'm sorry, just a moment, please (pause). Yes, [1] ... I help you?
A: Can you give me information about getting [2] ... London on the underground, please?
B: Well, here's a [3] ... showing the different lines.
A: Thank you. What about [4] ...? Are they expensive?
B: Mmm, it depends on the distance. But you can get a one-day travel card. They [5] ... three pounds ninety.
A: Thanks very much.

Listen and check your answers.

PRONUNCIATION

F

Copy the dialogue and listen again. Mark the intonation at the end of the sentences. Does it go up or down?

Example: A: Excuse me?
B: I'm sorry, just a moment please.

G

Work in pairs. Student A, imagine you are a tourist in your town. Student B, you work in the tourist information office. Act out this situation. Use the correct intonation!

A: Ask for help
B: Reply
A: Ask for information about buses
B: Give a map/timetable
A: Ask about the numbers of buses
B: Give information
A: Ask about price of tickets
B: Give information
A: Ask about times of buses
B: Give information
A: Say, 'Thanks very much.'

4 Going Out

A 🎟 KEYWORDS

Match the photos and the activities.

> going to a match skateboarding
> going to the cinema dancing
> eating out shopping

Example: A = going to the cinema

B ✏️

In pairs, make a list of things to do for young people where you live. Give names of places, times they are open and how to get there.

Example: Dancing: The Zone, young discotheque, open 5.00 - 9.00 p.m. Sat/Sun (bus)

Swimming: Olympic Pool, open 9.00 a.m. - 8.00 p.m. (underground)

C

Listen to Kath and Tim talking about their plans for the weekend. Copy and complete the diaries.

FRIDAY

| am | |
| pm | |

SATURDAY

| am | |
| pm | |

SUNDAY

| am | |
| pm | Visit Uncle Bill |

FRI:	am	
	pm	
SAT:	am	Clean room
	pm	
SUN:	am	
	pm	

Language Focus: Plans, intentions and arrangements

D LEARN TO LEARN

Match the rules with the examples.

1 We use the **infinitive** (or sometimes *no verb*) to write plans in a **diary**.
2 We use **going to** to talk about what we **intend** or **plan** to do in the future.
3 We use the **present continuous** to talk about definite **arrangements** we have made.

a I'm going to clean my room. It's in a terrible mess!
b Tonight I'm meeting Paul at 8 o'clock.
c uncle Bill *or* visit uncle Bill

E

Write five sentences about things you plan to do next weekend.

Example: I'm going to buy a new CD.

F

Write about this weekend in your diary. Include one *false* piece of information.

Example: Fri. 4 p.m. ~ go shopping in Avon Centre with Susan

G

'SPOT THE LIE' GAME

In pairs, ask what your partner is doing at the weekend and find out the false information.

Example: A: What are you doing on Friday afternoon?
B: At 4 o'clock I'm going shopping with Sue.
A: That's false! You don't finish school until 4.15!

H   DICTIONARY SKILLS

Use the mini-dictionary to check the stress of these adjectives.

afraid beautiful colourful crowded delicious impressive modern natural noisy romantic

Oo	Ooo	oO	oOo
famous	**dan**gerous	a**sleep**	ex**cit**ing
…	…	…	…
…	…	…	…
…	…		…

5 Fluency

A

Read this advice for listening to cassettes in class.

- Make sure you understand the task. Ask the teacher if you're not sure.
- Use the photos or pictures to make predictions about the tape.
- Predict what kind of language you need to listen for, e.g. numbers, times, activities
- Don't panic ~ the first time you listen, just try to get the general idea.

B 🔲

Look at the photos. Where do you think Larry and Jane live? Listen to the conversation and find out.

C 🔲

Copy the table. Listen again and complete it for Larry and Jane.

	LARRY	**JANE**
Going out		
Eating out		Pizza
At weekends	fishing /swimming	
After school		

Final Speaking Task: A Questionnaire

D

Read the questionnaire and write another similar question to find out if your partner is a city or country lover.

CITY SLICKER or Country Cat

1 YOU GO OUT FOR THE DAY IN THE COUNTRY. DO YOU:
   a) go for a long walk?
   b) find a nice place for a picnic?
   c) sit in the car and listen to your walkman?

2 YOU NEED TO GO INTO THE CITY CENTRE FOR SOMETHING. DO YOU:
   a) get angry with the people, traffic and pollution?
   b) get what you need, have a drink and go home?
   c) enjoy visiting as many shops as possible?

3 YOU WANT TO STUDY ENGLISH IN THE SUMMER. DO YOU:
   a) stay with a family in a village in Ireland?
   b) go to a summer school in a small town in the USA?
   c) go to an academy in the centre of London?

4 YOU'RE THINKING ABOUT A HOLIDAY BY THE SEA. DO YOU CHOOSE:
   a) an uninhabited island in Scotland?
   b) a small town on the north coast of France?
   c) a busy town like Benidorm?

KEY TO ANSWERS:
Mostly a) - you love nature and a quiet life; cities are too fast and dirty for you.
Mostly b) - you enjoy the good things about both cities and the country.
Mostly c) - you love the atmosphere and action in cities, but you find the country boring.

Now ask other students the questions and note their answers. Look at the key. Decide if they are city or country lovers and tell them.

Final Writing Task: A Tourist Brochure

E

City project

- **Read the brochure and find out which section mentions these things:**

old buildings / a football match / trams / pubs / museums / the airport / food / a rock concert

Example: old buildings - Places To See

- **What would *you* like to do in Manchester?**

- **Write a brochure for a city you know.**

Stage 1 Copy the four headings from the brochure and write interesting places and activities under each section for the city you have chosen.

Stage 2 Use your notes to write a brochure like the example above. Include adjectives (modern, fascinating, etc.)

Stage 3 Show your brochure to your partner and read his/hers. Can you find any mistakes?

Stage 4 Write a final version of your brochure. Add drawings or photos from magazines or postcards.

F

Listen to the song. Which of these places are mentioned?

Chicago / LA / St Louis / Oklahoma / Amarillo / New Mexico / New York / Missouri / New Orleans / San Francisco

MANCHESTER

HOW TO GET THERE: Manchester is located in the north-west of England. There are good rail and road communications and there is a busy international airport. There are modern trams in the centre and a good bus and train service to all areas of the city.

PLACES TO SEE: Manchester has something for everyone. There are some magnificent Victorian buildings near Albert Square. A visit to the Museum of Science and Industry gives a fascinating look into the past of this great city. Or why not take a bus to the Jodrell Bank Radio Telescope and Planetarium? If you like art, try the Whitworth Art Gallery - you'll find an impressive collection of modern and historic paintings and sculptures.

THINGS TO DO: Have fun in Manchester! Here are a few suggestions:
- go to a rock concert - remember, Simply Red and Oasis came from here
- watch a play at the Royal Exchange Theatre
- play some sport - there are lots of squash, tennis and golf clubs in the area
- watch a match at Old Trafford, home of Manchester United Football Club

EATING OUT: Manchester has a wonderful selection of international restaurants - Indian, Italian, Malaysian, Mexican... And if you like Chinese food, take a walk round Chinatown in the city centre. You can, of course, find good quality English food in most pubs!

For more information, visit the Tourist Information Office in Market Street.

6 Consolidation

Grammar

A

GUESS THE QUESTION

In groups, one person says an answer. The others have to guess the question.

Example: A: Saturday.
B: When do you play tennis?
C: When are you seeing your boyfriend?
D: What is your favourite day?

B

Put the words in the correct order to make questions.

1 is / which / near / river / Cairo?
2 what / is / capital / of / the / Italy?
3 Valencia / does / have / an / underground?
4 in / London / how / many / people / live?
5 you / do / at / go out / weekends?
6 when / they / did / the Eiffel Tower / build?

C

Write suitable questions for these answers.

1 On Sunday morning.
2 Yes, I do.
3 In the main square.
4 She's meeting her boyfriend.
5 No, it doesn't.
6 About 200,000.

D

Write five intentions for the school year.

Example: I'm going to speak English all the time in class.

E

Re-write the diary notes in full sentences.

Example: 1 My uncle is flying to London on Tuesday.

1 Tuesday: fly to London (*your uncle*)
2 Saturday night: meet Alex outside school. (*Ruth*)
3 Wednesday morning: maths exam (*we*)
4 Monday: start computer course (*I*)
5 Friday night: give history talk (*Sam and Dave*)

F LEARN TO LEARN

Look at the structures in the Language Check on page 22. Use the ideas below to organise your own grammar notes in your notebook.

1 Table

QUESTIONS			
What	do	you they	think
Where		she	live
When	does	it	get up

2 Timeline   **ARRANGEMENTS**

3 Translation *I am going to the cinema je vais au cinéma.*

Vocabulary

G LEARN TO LEARN

Which of these words are similar in your language? Check their meanings in the mini-dictionary and put new words in your vocabulary book.

shop pyramid airport restaurant pollution
map coffee traffic noise cinema crime
bicycle intention transport

H KEYWORDS

Put these verbs into the sentences.

get to / get around / get on / get up

1 I ... at 8 o'clock on school days.
2 It's difficult to ... a big city on a bicycle.
3 How do I ... the main square?
4 ... the number 12 bus near the museum.

I

MEMORY GAME

Play this game in groups. You have to add to the list.

Example:
A: In my city there is a museum.
B: In my city there is a museum and a cinema.
C: In my city there is a museum, a cinema and a big square.

Pronunciation

J

Copy the words. Then listen and mark the main stress.

Example: impressive, wonderful

impressive / wonderful / exciting / delicious / prosperous / powerful / historic / dangerous / expensive / romantic / beautiful

In pairs, practise saying the words in sentences about places you know.

Example: The White House is very impressive.
Italian food is delicious.

Test Yourself

A (7 points)
Write a question for the answers in italics.

1 There are *about 90* islands in Amsterdam.
2 *Ankara* is the capital of Turkey.
3 The Acropolis is *in Athens*.
4 *Yes,* they do speak French in Belgium.
5 Bilbao was founded *in 1300.*
6 *No,* Manchester doesn't have an underground.
7 The Great Mosque Hassan II is *in Casablanca.*

B (3 points)
What are these people's intentions?

1 Mark is often late for school. (*He is going to ...*)
2 I don't put my hand up in class. (*I ...*)
3 We don't try to speak English in class. (*We...*)

C (5 points)
Write Monica's diary notes in full sentences.

1 Saturday: morning - English homework
2   afternoon - shopping with Mum
3   evening - meet George 8.00 p.m. at cinema
4 Sunday: morning - tidy room
5   afternoon - lunch with Sam

D (5 points)
Put suitable words into the gaps.

1 The plane was late - we waited at the ... for two hours.
2 We wanted to ... the cathedral, so we looked at our ... .
3 In most cities the traffic ... are very bad.
4 We saw wonderful paintings in the art ... .

Extra Time

Look at Reading Club 1 on page 95.

Module Check

Language Check

QUESTIONS

Do you like big cities?
Does Manchester have an underground?
What is the capital of Holland?
Which river runs through Paris?
Where is St Paul's Cathedral?
When were the Olympics in Atlanta?
How many people are there in Brussels?
How do you get to school?
How long does it take you?

DIARY PLANS

Tuesday: meet Jan   Wednesday: science test

INTENTIONS

I am **going to** study a lot this term.
He is **going to** save money for a new stereo.

ARRANGEMENTS

I **am meeting** Paul outside the cinema.
My sister **is flying** to England next week.

Keyword Check

- **Make sure you know the meaning of these words and expressions.**
- **Put important new words in your vocabulary book.**

General: traffic jam, pollution, homeless, crime, litter, building, mountains, sea
Places: museum, cinema, disco, restaurant, park, art gallery, cathedral, airport, square
Free time: going to the cinema, dancing, shopping, eating out
Transport: bus, car, taxi, underground, bicycle, train, plane
Adjectives: impressive, fascinating, delicious, beautiful, expensive, romantic, powerful, wonderful
Opposites: dangerous/safe, poor/prosperous, ancient/modern, dirty/clean, noisy/quiet, exciting/boring
Asking for information: Excuse me? Can you give me information about ..., please? What about ...? Are they expensive?

- **Try to add more words to each list.**

Module diary

- **Which was your favourite lesson in module 1? Why?**
  Example: Lesson 1, City Quiz, because I like quizzes and games.

- **Write down something interesting or unusual from the module.**
  Example: In Tokyo, they push people onto the underground trains.

- **Which of these reading activities did you find the easiest?**
  - the great cities (Cairo, Paris and London)
  - global traffic jam
  - the brochure on Manchester

- **Did you try to participate in the speaking activities?**
  A a lot   B a little   C not very much

- **What was your score in the *Test Yourself*?**

- **Give yourself a mark for these structures:**
  - Questions
  - Plans and intentions
  A I understand them very well.
  B I sometimes make mistakes.
  C I don't understand them.

YESTERDAY

Lead-in

a KEYWORDS

Find these things in the photos.

sword horse steam train knight miner

b KEYWORDS

Copy the table and add more things from the past and present.

TRANSPORT	WEAPONS	JOBS
horse	sword	nurse
steam train	club	miner

c

**Play this game with your partner.
Take turns to say things from your table.
If you can't say anything, you're out of the game.**

Example: A: Transport - car.
  B: Steam train
  A: Boat

LEARN TO LEARN **Put new words in your vocabulary book.**

23

7 History Makers

Mother Teresa

Agnes Bojaxhiu [1] … born in Skopje in 1910. When Agnes was eighteen, she [2] … an Irish religious group. She [3] … the name 'Teresa' and [4] … to work in India. Starting in 1931, she [5] … geography and history at a school in Bengal for fifteen years. In 1946, she [6] … that she [7] … live and work with the poor. She [8] … an Indian citizen and she [9] … the rest of her life helping poor, old, sick, homeless and dying people in Calcutta. She [10] … the Nobel Peace Prize for her work in 1979. When she [11] … in 1997, at the age of eighty-seven, President Clinton [12] … 'We have lost one of the giants of our time.'

Language Focus: Past simple – Irregular verbs

A   KEYWORDS

Read the text and fill in the gaps. Use the verbs below in the past simple.

be / become / decide / die / go / join / have to / receive / say / spend / take / teach

Which verbs are regular? How do they end?

B

Read the text again. Copy and complete this table with dates and events in Mother Teresa's life.

DATE	EVENT
1910	Agnes Bojaxhiu was born.
…	…
…	…
…	…
…	…
1997	Mother Teresa died.

C

Listen to the story of another 'History maker'. Put these verbs in the order you hear them.

Example: 1 = see

pass / see / meet / start / arrive / want / crash

D

Listen again. Are these sentences true or false?

1 Amy was quite poor.
2 She flew to America.
3 She could speak German.
4 She repaired her aeroplane in India.

E

FAMOUS PEOPLE GAME

In groups, take turns to think of a famous person. The others ask questions to find out who it is. You can only answer 'yes' or 'no'.

Examples: Is it a man? Is he alive? Was he an artist? Did he play a sport? Was he from the USA?

You win if the others can't guess after ten questions.

F

Here are some more people who made history. Match the photos with the names and what they did.

a Marie Sklolowska Curie
b Nelson Mandela
c Rigoberta Menchu
d Mustafa Kemal Atatürk

1 A scientist who discovered the element radium.
2 He established the modern Turkish state.
3 He fought for democracy in South Africa.
4 She defended the rights of Central American people.

G

In pairs, take turns to test each other. Student A looks at number 2 on page 93 and Student B looks at number 2 on page 94.

Legends

THE SWORD IN THE STONE

SWORD·IS·THE·REAL·KING·OF

Pendragon, a brave but bad king, fell in love with a noble's wife. He decided to kill the noble ...¹... marry her. Some time ...²..., he and his wife had a baby son. Pendragon was afraid the nobles would kill his son, so he gave him to Merlin, the wizard. Merlin was clever and wise. He gave the baby to a knight. He didn't say the baby was Pendragon's son. The knight called the baby Arthur. Arthur played with the knight's son, Kay, and they grew up to be strong and healthy young men.

...³... a few years, King Pendragon died. Nobody knew about Arthur, and all the nobles wanted to be king. They fought for many years, ...⁴... one Christmas they decided to have a meeting in London to select a new king. ...⁵... they had the meeting, Merlin put a sword in a big stone next to the cathedral. He wrote a message on it: "The person who pulls out this sword is the real King of England."

Arthur and Kay went to London. Kay forgot his sword. Arthur went to look for it, but ...⁶... he could find it, he saw the sword in the stone. He thought it was Kay's sword and took it out!

...⁷... Kay saw the sword, he thought Arthur had stolen it, and ...⁸... told Arthur to put it back. Arthur put the sword back, ...⁹... Kay tried to pull it out, but he couldn't. Arthur ...¹⁰... pulled it out again!

...¹¹... the nobles heard about it, they didn't believe it. ...¹²... all this, Merlin explained that Arthur was King Pendragon's son, and Arthur became King of England.

A KEYWORDS

Which of these things can you see in the picture?

> sword   stone   knight   queen   message
> wizard   cathedral

B KEYWORDS

Read the first paragraph quickly and match these characters with the adjectives.

> healthy   wise   bad   clever   brave   strong

**MERLIN
THE WIZARD**   **YOUNG
ARTHUR**   **KING
PENDRAGON**

C

**Read the whole text more carefully.
Put these events in order.**

Example: 1 Pendragon gave Arthur to Merlin.

~ Pendragon died.
~ The nobles had a meeting in London.
~ Arthur grew up with Kay.
~ Arthur pulled the sword out of the stone.
~ Arthur became king.
~ Pendragon gave Arthur to Merlin

D

**Listen to the story and put these
words into the gaps in the text.**

when / after / and then /
immediately / before / later

E

**You are going to tell a story to another
student. Student A looks at number 3 on page
93. Student B looks at number 3 on page 94.
Both students follow the instructions below.**

1 Read the **notes** and use the mini-dictionary
   to check vocabulary.
2 When you tell the story, **use past tenses!**
3 **Practise** telling your story to yourself.
4 **Tell** your story to your partner - you can
   look at the timeline.

WILLIAM WALLACE

CLEOPATRA

Did you know?

Long ago, knights believed that a
sword, dipped in dragon's blood,
brought them good luck!

9 Memories

A

What is your earliest memory? Do you remember these things? Tell the class.

- Your first day at school.
- The first film you saw at the cinema.
- Your first holiday.

B

Claire is talking to her grandfather, Les Hanlon, about childhood memories. Who do you think says these sentences, Claire or Les?

1 The houses were very small.
2 I used to get up at half past six in the morning.
3 We used to have a really strict maths teacher.
4 I used to play outside all the time with my friends.
5 I got a job in a big house, as a domestic servant.
6 I used to help in our neighbours' shop on Saturdays.

Listen to the interview and check your predictions.

Language Focus: *Used to*

C

Look at the sentences in the box and then answer the questions.

> We *used to* have football matches.
> We *didn't use to* play outside in the streets.
> Where *did* you *use to* live?

1 How does the spelling of *used to* change in negatives and questions?
2 Does *used to* refer to past or present habits?
3 Explain the difference between: - I *used to* get up early - I *usually* get up early.

D

Think about when you were five or six years old. Compare what you did then with your life now. Write about each of these things:

- homework
- TV programmes
- bedtime
- sport

Example: I didn't use to have any homework, but now I have some every day. I used to go to bed at eight o'clock, but now I go much later.

E

Now write some questions to ask your partner.

Example: 1 = Did you use to have a lot of homework?

1 Did / have / a lot of homework?
2 What time / go to bed?
3 Which TV programmes / watch?
4 Which sports or game / play?

F

In pairs, find out the same information from your partner.

Example: A: Did you use to have a lot of homework?
B: No, I didn't use to have any homework.
A: And now?
B: Now I have homework every day.

G

Ask your teacher some questions about his/her childhood.

PRONUNCIATION

H

Listen to the six sentences. How many words are there in each sentence? Contractions, such as *what's*, count as two words.

Example: 1 = 7 words

Did you know?
Bhandanta Vicitsara recited 16,000 pages of Buddist text from memory in 1974.

10 Hard Times

A

In pairs, answer these questions.

1 What age can you leave school and get a job in your country?
2 When did your grandparents start work? Do you know their first jobs?
3 Have you ever worked at wee'
4 What job do you want to do when you finish your studies?

B

Read the reports from 1842 and match each one with the correct drawing.

1 When I was ten years old I went to work in a cotton mill. The mill owner used to like children as workers. We were cheap and he paid us very little. We were useful because we could climb under the machines and clean them. At our factory we used to start work at five o'clock in the morning. We never stopped work or sat down until nine or ten at night. Once, when I lost part of my finger in a machine, I bandaged it and went on working.

(BOY, ANONYMOUS)

2 I go down the mine at five in the morning and I come up at five at night. I work all night on Fridays and come away at twelve in the morning. I carry coal to the bottom of the mine. It usually weighs seven stones [1]. The distance varies, sometimes 300 yards [2], sometimes 500 yards [3]. I have to bend my back and legs, and the water often comes up to my knees. I don't like the work; my father makes me do it.

(JANET CUNNING, AGED ELEVEN)

[1] ABOUT **45** KILOS [2] ABOUT **277** METRES [3] ABOUT **461** METRES

3 When I was fourteen I started working for a family with nine children. I used to get up and light the fire, bath them and dress them, and get their breakfasts. Then I had to make the dinner and do all the washing up; and by that time, it would be teatime again. I had to put the children to bed, clean the rooms and prepare the fires for the next morning, and also the parents' supper. I wasn't in bed until twelve, and I had to get up by six.

(SUSY, A DOMESTIC SERVANT AGED SIXTEEN)

C

Now answer these questions.

1 How many hours a day did children work in cotton mills?
2 What time did Janet finish work on Saturdays?
3 How heavy was the coal that Janet carried?
4 How many hours did Susy work each day?
5 How many meals did Susy prepare every day?

D

Read the text again and answer these questions.

Example: 1 Sad and angry, because the conditions were terrible.

1 How did you feel when you read the reports? Sad, angry, happy? Why?
2 Why did mill owners like child workers?
3 Which do you think is the worst of the three jobs? Why?
4 Do you think the children knew how to read and write? Why or why not?

E KEYWORDS

Find the verbs in the text and match them with the definitions.

Example: 1 = c

1 went on (text 1)
2 come away (text 2)
3 comes up to (text 2)
4 get up (text 3)

a leave
b get out of bed
c continued
d reaches

F

In pairs, prepare your own list of rights for a 'Teenage Charter'. Think of some serious ones and some amusing ones. Write at least three rights and then read them to the class.

Example:

1 We think we should have a good education.
2 We believe young people should have free medical treatment.
3 We think we should have the right to play loud music late at night!

G

GUESS THE JOB

In groups, one student chooses a job from the past. The others ask questions to try and guess the job. You can only answer *yes*, *no* or *sometimes*.

Example jobs: miner / domestic servant / factory worker / tram driver / train driver / doctor / sailor / soldier / chimney sweep / farmer / nurse / scientist / teacher

Example questions: Did you work outside? Did you work with your hands? Did you use a machine? Did you travel in your job? Did you get dirty? Did you work with animals?

If the others don't guess after ten questions, you win.

H DICTIONARY SKILLS

The underlined words have more than one meaning. Look up the words in the mini-dictionary. Write the number of the appropriate meaning.

1 The light felt very <u>bright</u> after we came up from the mine.
2 William Wallace rested in the <u>country</u> after the battle.
3 The <u>plane</u> got to London at nine o'clock at night.
4 Always keep meat in the fridge so it doesn't go <u>bad</u>.
5 We used to eat a <u>light</u> meal before we went for a walk.
6 Bob Beamon <u>held</u> the world long jump record for more than 20 years.

11 Fluency

A

In pairs, Student A looks at number 4 on page 93. Student B looks at number 4 on page 94. Make notes for each heading of the network. You can use the mini-dictionary at the back of this book.

food

games

transport

name of
people

dates

location

weapons

B

Take turns to ask questions about your partner's civilisation.

Example: What did they eat?

NAME OF PEOPLE: What / name?
FOOD: What / eat?
TRANSPORT: How / travel?
LOCATION: Where / live?
WEAPONS: What / fight with?
DATES: When / live?
GAMES: What / play?

C

HISTORY QUIZ

- **Listen to the questions and try to answer them.**
- **In pairs, make up some more history questions to ask another pair.**

Final Writing Task: A Biography

Write about the life of Albert Einstein.

1879 ○ is born in Ulm, Germany

○ doesn't talk until the age of three!

1891 ○ teaches himself geometry!

1894 ○ family moves to Milan

1900 ○ teachers don't recommend him for university!

1903 ○ gets married

1905 ○ writes the Special Theory of Relativity

1922 ○ wins the Nobel Prize for physics

1933 ○ leaves Germany when Hitler comes to power

1939 ○ writes to the President of the USA about the possibility of building an atomic bomb

1945 ○ after the war speaks against nuclear weapons

1955 ○ dies in the USA

Stage 1 Read about Einstein and write sentences in the past tense.

Stage 2 Join some of the sentences with these words: *when, later, after, before, immediately, and then.*

Stage 3 Divide the information into three parts: early life; what made him famous; later life.

Stage 4 Write a short biography in three paragraphs.

Final Speaking Task: A Life Story

• **In groups of three, think of a famous person you know some information about. Don't worry about exact dates.**

• **Draw a timeline and write notes about the person's life.**

Example: – 1962 – is born in ...

– 1982 – first part in TV film ...

– 1985 – marries .....

• **Divide your information into three parts:**
  – early life and what made him/her famous
  – later life
  – what he/she is doing now

• **Each student in the group talks about one part of the person's life.**
Prepare sentences, then check your tenses with the Irregular verb list on page 112.

• **Practise telling your part of the life story to the group. Do *not* say the name of the person.**

• **Tell your life story to another group or to the whole class. The others have to guess the person.**

33

12 Consolidation

Grammar

A

Put the verbs in brackets into the past simple tense.

Joan of Arc ...¹... (be) born in France in 1412. As a young girl, she ...²... (begin) to hear voices. She ...³... (think) they ...⁴... (be) the voices of saints.

She ...⁵... (say) the voices ...⁶... (tell) her to attack the English army that was in France. She ...⁷... (reorganise) the French army and ...⁸... (win) a famous battle at Orléans. Later, Joan's sword ...⁹... (break) in a battle near Paris. Her soldiers ...¹⁰... (see) this as a sign of bad luck and ...¹¹... (not want) to follow her any more. Finally, the English ...¹²... (capture) Joan and ...¹³... (kill) her in 1431. After her death, Joan ...¹⁴... (become) a national heroine. She was ...¹⁵... (make) a saint in 1920.

B

Rewrite each sentence using the correct form of *used to*.

Example: 1 I didn't *use to* like cheese.

1 I didn't like cheese when I was young. Now I love it!
2 I lived in a small village before I came to the city.
3 She studied hard last year, but now she goes out every night.
4 Many years ago, that man was very poor.
5 Where did you go on holiday when you were young?

C

In groups, imagine it is the year 2050. Take turns to talk about your teenage memories. Talk about school, hobbies, family, music, sport, holidays, etc.

Example: A: When I was fifteen I used to like techno music.
B: I didn't. I used to like heavy metal.

Vocabulary

D

Copy and complete this table.

NOUN	ADJECTIVE
health	...
...	democratic
bravery	...
anger	...
...	strong

E

Replace the verbs in italics with these verbs in the correct form.

go on / grow up /come up to

1 The water in the pool *reaches* my shoulders.
2 Les Hanlon *spent his childhood* in an orphanage.
3 He *continued* fighting for many years.

F KEYWORDS

Match the verbs with the objects.

Example: 1 = c

1	ride	**a**	the dinner
2	drive	**b**	a bus
3	make	**c**	a bike
4	do	**d**	TV
5	watch	**e**	a car
6	catch	**f**	the washing-up

G

VOCABULARY GAME

- **Look at the first two modules of the book or your vocabulary book and find ten new words.**
- **Write each word in *your* language on a small piece of paper.**
- **In groups, mix up all the pieces of paper. Take turns to choose a word. If you know it in English, you get a point. If you don't know it, write it in your vocabulary book.**

Pronunciation

H 🎞️

Listen to the different ways you can pronounce the letter 'i'.

Group 1	Group 2	Group 3
/ aɪ / time	/ ɪ / big	/ ɜː / girl

Copy the sentences and mark each letter 'i' 1, 2 or 3. Then listen and check your answers.

Example: 1 = They didn't find the rich girl.

1 They didn't find the rich girl.
2 First King Pendragon killed a noble.
3 Then his wife had a baby, Arthur.
4 After this, they gave him to Merlin, the wise wizard.

Test Yourself

A (15 points)

Put the verbs in brackets in the past simple tense. If there is also a star (*), use a suitable form of *used to* with the verb.

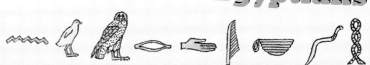

The Ancient Egyptians [1]... (begin) a great empire on the river Nile over 5,000 years ago. We know a lot about them because they [2]... (*write) everything down using a system of picture signs called 'hieroglyphics'. They [3]... (write) on stones and also [4]... (invent) a type of paper made from papyrus, a plant which [5]... (grow) on the Nile. They [6]... (*sail) boats up the Nile to Nubia to get gold, perfume, and Nubian beer, which was a favourite drink. They [7]... (not *sail) as much on the 'Great Green' (their name for the sea) but sometimes [8]... (go) on the Mediterranean and the Red Sea. They [9]... (exchange) corn and wine for wood and animal skins. In their own markets, they [10]... (not *pay) with metal money, but [11]... (buy) things with shells. Egyptians were the first people to build large stone buildings called pyramids. When important people [12]... (die), they [13]... (put) them in a pyramid. They also [14]... (make) huge statues like the Sphinx and we know that they [15]... (understand) advanced mathematics.

B (5 points)

Put suitable words into the gaps.

1 The Vikings sailed in long ... all over Europe.
2 Knights rode on ... and fought with ... .
3 A hundred years ago, many people worked as domestic ... .
4 Einstein was a great ... .

Extra Time

Look at Reading Club 2 on page 96.

Module Check

Language Check

PAST SIMPLE

Regular verbs
The Vikings **sailed** in wooden boats.
They **didn't sail** to Australia.
Did they **sail** to America?

Irregular verbs
Amy Johnson **flew** to Australia.
She **didn't fly** around the world.
Did she **fly** back home?

USED TO
They **used to** pay children very little.
They **didn't use to** have a good education.
Did you **use to** play with dolls?

Keyword Check

- Make sure you know the meaning of these words and expressions.
- Put important new words in your vocabulary book.

Jobs: nurse, miner, factory worker, farmer, doctor, teacher, scientist
Transport: car, motorbike, bicycle, train, bus, tram, plane, boat
Adjectives/Nouns: free/freedom, brave/bravery, healthy/health, democratic/democracy, angry/anger, wise/wisdom, scientific/science, dangerous/danger
Verbs: go on, get up, come up to, come away, grow up, pull out
Giving opinions: I think we should have ..., We believe young people should have ...
Verbs/Nouns: win a battle, go to school, have a meeting, get a job, do homework, make the lunch

- Try to add more words to each list.

Module diary

- **Who do you think was the most interesting person in this module?**
  Example: For me, Einstein. I think he was a great man.
- **Which of these listening activities did you find the easiest?**
  - The life of Amy Johnson
  - The King Arthur story
  - The memories of Les and Claire Hanlon
  - The history quiz
- **Look at your writing from modules 1 and 2. Which was your favourite activity?**
  - brochure about your town/city
  - biography of Einstein

- **What was your score in the *Test Yourself*?**
- **Give yourself a mark for these structures:**
  - Past simple
  - *Used to*
  A I understand them very well.
  B I sometimes make mistakes.
  C I don't understand them.
- **Vocabulary questionnaire.**
  - How many new words have you written down from this module?
  - Do you give a translation in your own language?
  - Do you put the words in an example sentence?

NATURE

Lead-in

a KEYWORDS

Use the mini-dictionary to check the meaning of the words in italics in the questionnaire.

b

In pairs, ask and answer the questions about *your* region.

Example: A: When do leaves start growing on the trees?
B: In March or April.

c 📼

Listen to extracts from *The Four Seasons* by Vivaldi. Which seasons are the extracts about?

Nature Watch

1 In which month do these things happen?
• *Leaves* start growing on the trees in spring
• *Migrating* birds arrive in your area
• Birds and animals start *breeding*
• Leaves start *falling* in autumn

2 Which of these species of wildlife can you find?
• bear / wolf / lynx / bat
• flamingo / eagle / vulture
• shark / salmon / whale

3. Which of these *habitats* can you find?
• mountains / sea / rivers / lakes / plains / forests / rain forests

13 Wonders of Nature

A

🔑 KEYWORDS

Match the adjectives with the animals in the photos.

> deadly beautiful delicate strange sleepy thin slow dangerous

Example: Centipede = strange, thin

NOT TOO FAST

The loris is not the most active animal in the world. It lives and sleeps in the rainforests of South Asia. It is careful and deliberate when it climbs. It doesn't swing or jump like a monkey. That is too energetic! Lorises are small and brown and have very large eyes because they feed at night on insects and plants. They also like small birds but they don't catch many! They are one of the slowest and sleepiest animals in the rainforest.

THE TERRIBLE SMILE OF THE GREAT WHITE

The shark has always had a bad reputation and the Great White (the star of the film *Jaws*), has the worst of all. It is the most dangerous shark that exists and perhaps the deadliest assassin of the animal kingdom. It swims near beaches and has killed many people. With its impressive teeth it can bite through cables and boats! The biggest white sharks are up to six metres long and weigh up to 1800 kilos.

FEEDING FROM A FLOWER IN MEXICO

Perhaps the most beautiful and delicate bird in the world is the hummingbird. Hummingbirds are tiny, brightly coloured creatures which live in forests and feed on the nectar of flowers. The smallest of all is the bee hummingbird which only weighs two grams. Hummingbirds can hover in the air, just like helicopters, moving their wings up to 200 times per second.

B

Read the texts and choose one of these titles for each text:

- Lots of legs
- Nature's helicopter
- Energy saver
- Deadly assassin

C

Look at the network for a centipede. Complete networks for the other animals.

worms and insects — food

dark, wet places — habitat

centipede

colour — brown/grey

size — usually less than 10cm long

COUNT MY FEET

With its busy little legs and long thin body, the centipede is one of the strangest common insects. Centipedes can be brown or grey. They love dark, wet places and eat worms and insects. Most centipedes are less than ten centimetres long but the giant centipede from Madagascar, the world's longest centipede, can reach 30 centimetres! "Centipede" means "one hundred feet". Is that a good name?

Language Focus: Comparatives and superlatives

D

Copy and complete the tables with the words from the lists below. The texts will also help you.

SHORT ADJECTIVES

| thin | thinner | the thinnest |

thin / big / small / deadly / strange / light / tiny

IRREGULAR ADJECTIVES

| good | better | the best |

good / bad

LONG ADJECTIVES

| dangerous | more dangerous | the most dangerous |
| dangerous | less dangerous | the least dangerous |

interesting / delicate

E

Guess which animal this description is about. Then put the adjectives in the correct form.

> This animal is ¹... (small) than a whale but ²... (big) than a hummingbird. It is one of the ³... (large) land animals in the world, after the African elephant and possibly the hippopotamus. Its legs are ⁴... (short) than a giraffe's but its body is ⁵... (heavy) and it has a very big head with one or two horns. It is ⁶... (slow) than a lion or cheetah but it is ⁷... (fast) than a sloth. It is ⁸... (dangerous) than a lion or tiger but is ⁹... (dangerous) than a hippopotamus. It is not the ¹⁰... (delicate) animal in the world. Now it is in real danger of extinction.

F

Choose an animal and write a similar description. Then, in pairs, read out your description. See if your partner can guess the animal.

G  DICTIONARY SKILLS

Use the mini-dictionary to complete the table about these verbs. If there is no information, the verb is regular.

VERB	PRESENT PARTICIPLE	PAST
	biting	
		died
fall		
		beat
		weighed
	noticing	
smash		

14 Endangered Species

A

Copy this table and add to the list of wildlife that is in danger of extinction.

WORLD	MY COUNTRY
tigers	bears

Read the first paragraph of the article and add more animals to your list.

B

Read the rest of the article and answer the questions.

1 How big are tigers?
2 What do they eat?
3 How many wild tigers are there now?
4 How have conservationists tried to save tigers?
5 Why are tigers disappearing?

C  KEYWORDS

Copy and complete the sentences.

1 Weight: Tigers can ... up to 225 kilos.
2 Length: Tigers can be 3 metres ...
3 Height: Tigers are over 1 metre ...
4 Colour: Tigers have orange ... with black or brown ...
5 Food: Tigers ... animals like wild pigs or antelopes.

GOING, GOING... GONE.

Today there are many species which are very close to extinction: the beluga whale, the giant panda, the grey wolf, the African black rhino and the gorilla. However, perhaps the most spectacular of all animals in danger of extinction is the magnificent tiger, the largest cat on the planet.

Tigers can be up to 4 metres long and over a metre high, weighing up to 225 kilos and they have beautiful orange fur with black or brown stripes. They hunt animals like wild pigs, deer and buffalo and can eat as much as 40 kilos of meat in one meal.

Fifty years ago there were between 25,000 and 30,000 tigers in Asia but this number has fallen to between 5,000 and 7,000. Since the 1980s, the conservation programme 'Operation Tiger' has tried to save the Indian tiger by establishing national parks or reserves.

Unfortunately, the tiger's body is in enormous demand for traditional Chinese medicine and illegal hunters can get up to $20,000 for a dead tiger. Also their habitat is disappearing because poor farmers are cutting wood at reserves like Ranthambhore National Park in India. If we cannot stop the hunting or protect its habitat, in the next few years this great cat will disappear forever.

D

Read the description and then copy and complete the table.

The hippopotamus lives near rivers in tropical areas of Africa. It is one of the biggest mammals, about 150 cm high and nearly three and a half metres long. It weighs around 3,500 kilos. The hippo has dark skin, a very big body and small eyes and ears.

It lives in groups of 15-20 females and young with one dominant male. The hippo is not aggressive. It spends the day in water and comes out at night to look for grass, plants and fruit. Baby hippos are often born in the water after a gestation period of 230 days. Hippos are not an endangered species, but the population is much smaller than before.

habitat: *rivers/lakes in tropical Africa*
size:
physical characteristics:
behaviour: *lives in groups 10-15 with 1 dominant male / not aggressive / during day lives in water / looks for food at night*
food:
breeding: *often born in water / gestation period - 230 days*
population:

E

Student A looks at number 5 on page 93. Student B looks at number 5 on page 94. Use the notes to write a description like the one in exercise D.

F

In pairs, ask and answer the following questions about your animals. Complete a table like the one in exercise D.

Where does it live? How big is it? What does it look like? How does it behave? What does it eat? What breeding habits does it have? What is the population?

Did you know?
The best-known extinct creature is the dodo, which disappeared in 1681. It had blue-grey feathers and very small useless wings.

Your Planet Needs You

A

In pairs, look at the photos and match them with the questions below. Then try to answer the questions.

1 What everyday objects can we recycle?
2 What causes air pollution and acid rain?
3 Which of the world's seas are the most polluted?
4 What is happening to the world's rain forests?
5 What destroys the ozone layer?
6 What is happening to the world's climate?

B

Check your answers by reading this leaflet.

FRIENDS OF THE EARTH IS FIGHTING ON THESE ISSUES:

 RECYCLING
We can still do more to recycle glass, paper, cans and plastic.

 AIR POLLUTION
Pollution from factories and cars poisons the air we breathe and causes acid rain, which kills our trees.

 WATER POLLUTION
Many of our seas, like the North Sea and the Mediterranean, are full of chemicals and sewage.

 SAVING THE RAIN FOREST
In Brazil's rain forests an area roughly the size of England and Wales is destroyed every year.

 THE OZONE LAYER
Chemicals like the CFCs found in fridges are damaging the ozone layer.

 THE GREENHOUSE EFFECT
The world's temperature is going up and the climate is changing.

C

Listen to the interview with Alison. Which of the problems in the leaflet does she mention?

Example: the rain forests

D

Listen again. Complete the questionnaire for Alison in your notebook.

How green are YOU?

1 **What do you do to recycle things?**
  Collect newspapers / use recycled paper
2 **What do you do to save energy?**
3 **What do you do to help animals and wildlife?**
4 **Are you and your family green shoppers?**

E

In pairs, use the questionnaire above to find out how 'green' your partner is.

F

Make a list of practical ways that we can help the planet. Think about some of the things below.

paper / electricity / tins / bottles / petrol / animals / birds / food / shopping / gardens / pets / trees / rivers / the sea

Example: We should always write on both sides of the paper to save paper. We shouldn't leave lights on and waste electricity.

16 Takuana Island

A LEARN TO LEARN

When you listen to cassettes in class, which of these things do you do?

- Before listening, I think about the topic and make predictions.

- When I am not sure about the questions, I ask the teacher.
- When I do not understand very much, I don't panic. I continue listening.
- I try to listen for important words.

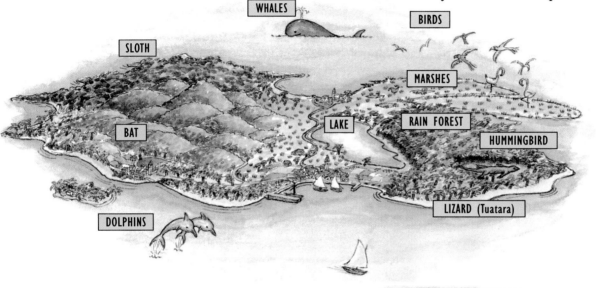

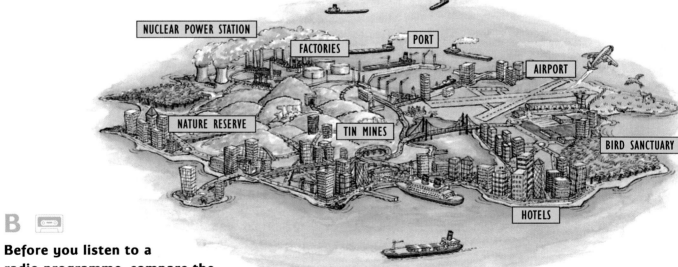

B 📼

Before you listen to a radio programme, compare the two drawings and check the vocabulary. What subjects do you think the programme will mention?

- birds and animals
- factories and mines

- destruction of rain forests
- famous people from Takuana
- Takuana cooking

- pollution
- the Taku language

Listen and check your answers.

Language Focus: Conditional sentences (1)

C

Listen again. Match the two parts of the sentences.

Example: 1 = c

1 If we build an airport in the marshes,
2 What will happen to the island
3 If they build a port,
4 If thousands of people come to the island,
5 If they destroy the rain forest,

a the climate will change.
b they will pollute the sea.
c many species of birds will disappear.
d if they do that?
e the Taku language will disappear.

D

Look at the conditional sentences in exercise C again. Which tenses are used? Copy and complete the chart.

CONDITION	CONSEQUENCE
If +......... tense	+......... tense

Did you know?
Every year an average person in Britain uses paper made from <u>six</u> trees!

E

Use the words below to write sentences about Takuana.

Example: If they develop the island, there will be better schools and hospitals.

1 develop island / be better schools and hospitals
2 more jobs / people be more prosperous
3 build hospitals / people be healthier
4 make nature reserves / protect wildlife
5 build hotels / tourists come to island
6 mine tin / destroy rain forests
7 destroy rain forest / wildlife disappear
8 build factories / cause pollution

F

PRONUNCIATION

Listen to six sentences. Write down the most important words.

Example: 1 If / destroy / rain forest / climate / change

Listen again and repeat the sentences.

G

CONDITIONAL GAME

Think of five conditional sentences. Write conditions on small pieces of paper and consequences on others. In groups, mix up the papers. Take turns to match your partners' sentences.

Example: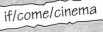

buy/you/coffee
if/come/cinema
if/rains
stay/at home

Example: A: If it rains, I will buy you a coffee.
B: No!
A: If it rains, I will stay at home.
B: Yes!

A

Listen and match the descriptions with the drawings.

Taku Wildlife Quiz

- **Taku bat**
- **Yellow-headed dolphin**
- **Tuatara**
- **Taku hummingbird**

One of the animals above really exists (with another name). Which is it?

B

The letter below to the *Taku Herald* is from the company that wants to mine tin. Match the topics with the paragraphs.

- the advantages of the plan
- reasons for writing the letter
- public meeting
- pollution and conservation

National Tin Corporation
10 Stamford Road,
London EC2

2 May

Dear Sir/Madam,

1 I am writing to explain the development plans for Takuana. Many people are worried because "green" groups are giving out false information.

2 The island is pretty, but it is one of the poorest places in the world. If we start mining, there will be more jobs for the people of Takuana and they will have new houses, hospitals, schools, roads and sports facilities.

3 There will be some pollution, but much less than the "greens" say. Mines and factories will have strict pollution controls and the nuclear power station will not pollute the air. We will protect all the rare animals on the island in nature reserves and bird sanctuaries.

4 In my opinion, the new development will bring progress and prosperity to the island. I will be in Taku City next month to attend the public meeting and I look forward to discussing the plan with the people of Takuana then.

Yours faithfully,

Phei Chang

(Chief executive NTC)

C

Read the letter again and match the expressions with when they are used.

Example: 1 = d

1	*In my opinion, ...*	**a**	start letter formally
2	*Yours faithfully,*	**b**	explain why you are writing
3	*I look forward to discussing ...*	**c**	contrast ideas
4	*The island is pretty, but ...*	**d**	express an opinion
5	*I am writing to explain ...*	**e**	talk about a future event
6	*Dear Sir/Madam,*	**f**	finish a formal letter

Final Writing Task: An Ecological Project

D

Now write a project about an ecological problem in your area.

Stage 1 Think about an ecological problem in your area.

Stage 2 Gather information:
  • Discuss the problem with a friend
  • Try to find a newspaper article about the problem
  • Find (or draw) a picture to show the problem
  • Gather opinions about the problem
    (e.g. interview classmates, friends or your parents about it)

Stage 3 Write notes to:
  • give your reasons for choosing this problem
  • describe the problem and its causes
  • describe how some local people feel about the problem
  • suggest how we can solve the problem

Stage 4 Complete your project:
  • Write a short introduction
  • Make a contents page
  • Write your project

E

Nature project

In groups, produce a poster or magazine.

• Collect pieces of writing you have done in this module.
• Add some things: photos, drawings, leaves, etc. to illustrate your project.

Final Speaking Task: A Debate

F

• **Form six groups:**
  • students from Takuana
  • ecological groups
  • local Taku business people
  • local farmers
  • executives from NTC
  • representatives of other foreign businesses

• **Decide if you are in favour of the plan or against it and list your reasons. You can also think of an alternative plan.**

• **One member of each group reports to the class.**

Example: "We are in favour of the plan, because we think that ..."

• **Vote and see if the class decides to accept or reject the plan.**

18 Consolidation

Grammar

A

Read the descriptions and work out the names of the dogs.

Ivor is bigger than his sister Colly but his ears are shorter. His hair is thicker than his other brother Leif and he has more black hair than his sister. Ivor is a better hunter than his other brother and sister and he has

stronger teeth and a longer nose than his brother Leif. Leif is smaller than his brother but he is more intelligent. He has longer ears than his sister and he has more white fur than her. Colly is smaller than Leif and her ears

are shorter, but she has a longer nose than her brother Ivor. Her fur is thicker than Ivor's and she has bigger eyes than him. She is the most intelligent and she can understand thirty words!

B

Order the words to make sentences.

Example: 1 = If we destroy more forests in Europe, the European brown bear will disappear.

1 we / the European brown bear / more forests / If / destroy / in Europe / will disappear
2 some islands / the world temperature / will disappear / If / goes up / in the Indian Ocean
3 like Chernobyl / nuclear power / there will be / another / to use / If / we continue / accident
4 will / our forests / paper / we do not / If / we / recycle / destroy
5 in our cities / get worse / if / more cars / Air pollution / we have / will

Vocabulary

C KEYWORDS

Copy and complete the table below.

NOUNS	ADJECTIVES	NOUNS	ADJECTIVES
intelligence	...	extinction	...
...	long	danger	...
height	...	...	polluted

D KEYWORDS

Copy and complete the words below. One word or two?

Example: 1 wildlife (1 word)
2 acid rain (2 words)

1 wild ... 2 acid ... 3 humming ... 4 vampire ...
5 rain ... 6 ozone ... 7 stick ... 8 giant ... 9 news ...
10 light ... 11 carbon ... 12 power ...

48

E

VOCABULARY GAME

In pairs, see how many names of animals you can put into a word chain. The last letter of one word becomes the first letter of the next. The pair with the longest chain is the winner!

Example: zebr<u>a</u>ntelop<u>e</u>lephan<u>t</u>iger<u>a</u>t

Pronunciation

F

Listen to some of the different ways you can pronounce the letter 'o'.

Group 1	Group 2	Group 3
not /ɒ/	some /ʌ/	so /əʊ/

Which group do these words belong to?

long / month / hot / does / grow / come / cold / forest / slow / one / over / orange / jobs

Example: long = Group 1

Test Yourself

A   (15 points)

Put the words in brackets in the correct form.

A: Have you heard about the new power station they're going to build?

B: Yes, I think it's a good idea. If they ¹... (build) the power station, we ²... (have) some jobs in this town at last. And if there ³... (be) a power station, other industries ⁴... (come) here.

A: But what about the pollution? We have pollution now, and with a power station it will get ⁵... (bad). If they ⁶... (build) it near the river, they ⁷... (pollute) that too. Now our river is one of the ⁸... (good) places for fishing in the area.

B: I think that jobs are ⁹... (important) than pollution. Most of our young people go to London to work. The population is growing ¹⁰... (old) every year!

A: I don't agree.

B: Well, it's OK for you. You have a job. But what about young people? If there ¹¹... (be) more jobs, we ¹²... (get) more schools and maybe a new hospital.

A: But with a power station there will be more traffic, so the roads will become ¹³... (dangerous). If we ¹⁴... (not protect) our town, it ¹⁵... (become) a horrible place to live in.

B   (5 points)

Complete the sentences below.

1 They are destroying a lot of the *rain* ... in the world.
2 The *wild* ... in that country is disappearing very quickly.
3 The factories are causing *acid* ... in our area.
4 We need to recycle things like *news* ...
5 He's got a new pet which looks really strange. It's a *stick* ...

Extra Time

Look at Reading Club 3 on page 97.

Language Check

COMPARISON

Short Adjectives

The centipede is **thinner than** the snake.
It is one of **the thinnest** insects in the world.
The hummingbird is **smaller** than many other birds.
The bee hummingbird is **the smallest** of all birds.
The white shark is **deadlier than** the tiger.
It is **the deadliest** creature on earth.

Long Adjectives

The humming bird is **more beautiful than** other birds.
It is one of **the most beautiful** birds there is.

Irregular Adjectives

Black bears are **better** climbers **than** brown bears, but **the best** climbers in the bear family are sun bears from Asia.

CONDITIONALS (1)

If they destroy the rain forest, the climate **will change**.
If we **don't protect** the Taku sloth, it **will disappear**.
What **will happen** to the island, **if** we **do** that?

Keyword Check

- **Make sure you know the meaning of these words and expressions.**
- **Put important new words in your vocabulary book.**

Seasons: spring, summer, autumn, winter
Animals: centipede, loris, white shark, hummingbird, hippopotamus, tiger, whale, vulture, flamingo, rhino, wolf, lynx, wild boar, gorilla
Habitats: plains, forests, lakes, rivers, mountains,
Environment: wildlife, recycling, pollution, acid rain, rain forest, ozone layer, save, waste
Compound nouns: *one word:* wildlife, hummingbird, lightbulb, newspaper
two words: acid rain, rain forest, carbon dioxide, power station
Nouns/adjectives: length/long height/high extinction/extinct prosperity/prosperous
Expressing opinions: I'm in favour of ..., I'm against ..., I think we should ...
Descriptions: How big is it? What does it look like? It weighs ..., It's got dark skin and a pink face.

- **Try to add more words to each list.**

Module diary

- **Which was your favourite lesson in module 3? Why?**
  Example: I liked Wonders of Nature, because I love wildlife.
- **Which animal from this module did you find most interesting?**
  Example: The grey wolf, because it is strong!
- **How well do you understand the following?**
  - your partners in class
  - cassettes you listen to
  - the teacher's explanations
  - pop songs

  A I understand them well.
  B I get the general idea.
  C I only understand a few words.

- **Give yourself a mark for speaking in class.**
  A I have problems but I can communicate.
  B I have a lot of problems but I try to communicate.
  C I don't try to speak English.
- **What was your score in the *Test Yourself*?**
- **Give yourself a mark for:**
  - comparative and superlative adjectives
  - conditionals (1)

  A I understand them very well.
  B I sometimes have problems.
  C I don't understand them.

- **How many new words have you learnt in this module?**

  A more than twenty B more than ten C less than five

FANTASY

Lead-in

a   KEYWORDS

Match these sentences with the photos.

1 In Britain there are many <u>haunted</u> <u>places</u> where <u>ghosts</u> sometimes appear.
2 Some people with <u>special powers</u> can <u>levitate</u> or <u>firewalk</u>.
3 <u>Werewolves</u> are people who <u>turn into</u> wolves during a <u>full moon</u> and attack humans.
4 <u>Vampires</u> drink the <u>blood</u> of living victims.

b

Use the mini-dictionary to check the underlined words.

c

In pairs, find out if your partner believes the things above exist. Use the expressions below.

Example: A: What do you think about vampires?
          B: I'm sure ...

I'm sure they don't exist. / I think they may exist. / I'm sure they exist.

51

The Unexplained

A

Read the sentences below. Which do you think are possible?

Example: I think number one is possible. I'm sure number two isn't possible.

1 to walk across fire without getting burnt
2 to move or bend objects without touching them
3 to dream something before it happens
4 to communicate telepathically with another person
5 to levitate

B

Read the article. Match each paragraph with the experiences in exercise A.

C

Read the text again. True or false?

1 Some people can firewalk without getting burnt.
2 Subbayah Pullavar was a great firewalker.
3 Uri Geller levitated on television.
4 Some people have levitated or bent objects.
5 Telepaths can only "communicate" with their family or close friends.

SPECIAL POWERS

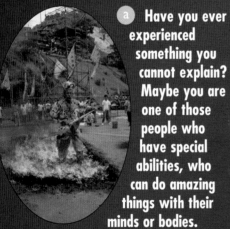

a Have you ever experienced something you cannot explain? Maybe you are one of those people who have special abilities, who can do amazing things with their minds or bodies. For example, many people have walked across fires without getting burnt. In 1935 the incredible Indian firewalker, Kuda Bux, walked across a fire at a temperature of 1400°C. Later he had <u>no</u> burns on his feet.

b There have also been many curious cases of levitation. In 1936 an Indian mystic Subbayah Pullavar began to float in the air. He was photographed and people passed their hands under his body to make sure he was not supported.

c Many psychics have made objects move without touching them. The Israeli, Uri Geller, appeared on television a few years ago and bent forks and spoons. There was also a Polish woman who moved small objects like scissors without touching them.

d Other people have the mysterious ability to get information without using the ordinary five senses. For example, telepathic people can communicate with other people, and scientists have written about many cases of telepathy amongst family or close friends. There are also people who have had strange premonitions and "seen" the future in their dreams.

D

Which of these adjectives from the text are similar in your language?

> special amazing incredible curious
> mysterious telepathic strange

Language Focus: Present perfect/past simple

E

Look at the sentences. Are they past simple or present perfect?

a Many people have walked across fires without getting burnt.

b In 1935 Kuda Bux walked across a fire at a temperature of 1400°C.

c Have you ever experienced something you cannot explain?

d There have been many curious cases of levitation.

e In 1936 Indian mystic, Subbayah Pullavar, began to float in the air.

· **Which sentence above is about personal experiences in the past?**
· **Which tense do we use to describe an event in the past:**
  i without a specific time?
  ii with a specific time?

F

Find the past participles in the text for the verbs below. Which are irregular?

experience walk be see make write have

G

Read the text and put the verbs in brackets in the past simple or present perfect.

Example: 1 have always been

> People ¹... (always be) curious about the future. Some people ²... (predict) the future. Michel de Nostradamos ³... (make) 1,000 predictions between 1555 and 1566. Up to now many of these predictions ⁴... (come) true. Other people ⁵... (have) premonitions in dreams. They ⁶... (dream) about real events days or weeks before they have happened.
> For example, in 1974 a man from Ohio, USA ⁷... (dream) about a terrible air disaster at Chicago airport. A few days later an identical accident ⁸... (happen) killing 275 people.

H

TELEPATHY GAME

In pairs, one person slowly writes down 5 numbers between 1-10. The other person concentrates and tries to guess what the numbers are. When you have finished, see how many numbers you guessed. If you get more than 3, you may be telepathic!

Fact or fantasy?

In the 19th century there was an Italian woman who could read with her ears. Many other people can read with their fingers.

(Check your answers on page 111.)

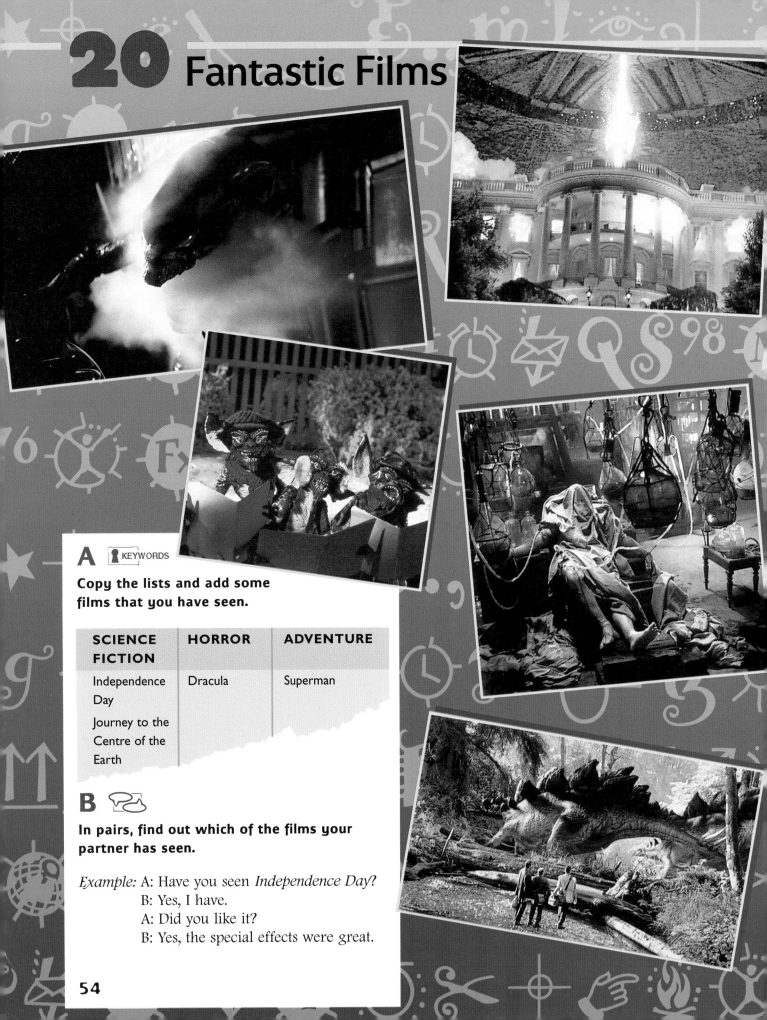

20 Fantastic Films

A 🔑 KEYWORDS

Copy the lists and add some films that you have seen.

SCIENCE FICTION	HORROR	ADVENTURE
Independence Day	Dracula	Superman
Journey to the Centre of the Earth		

B 💬

In pairs, find out which of the films your partner has seen.

Example: A: Have you seen *Independence Day*?
B: Yes, I have.
A: Did you like it?
B: Yes, the special effects were great.

E

Plan your diary for next week. Include three things that you often do.

	afternoon	evening
Monday		
Tuesday		
Wednesday	swimming lesson 4 p.m.	
Thursday		
Friday		judo class
Saturday	go skateboarding in park	
Sunday		

F

In groups, invite people to go with you to see a film.

Example: A: Would you like to come and see *Alien* on Wednesday afternoon?

B: I'm sorry, I'm busy. I'm going swimming.

A: Let's go and see *Frankenstein* on Wednesday evening then.

B: OK, that's a good idea. What time shall we meet?

A: How about meeting at eight o'clock outside the cinema?

Write down the films you arrange to see in your diary, like this:

> Frankenstein 8 p.m. with Sandra

C

Listen to the two dialogues. Answer these questions.

1 What film did Sue and Dave go and see?
2 When did Kate and Richard go to the cinema?
3 What film did they decide to see?
4 When and where did they arrange to meet?

D

Listen to the first dialogue again and complete it.

SUE: I feel like going out this afternoon. [1]... we go to the cinema?

DAVE: There's nothing on at the moment.

SUE: Yes, there is. [2]... go and see *Gremlins*? It's a brilliant film. I really want to see it again.

DAVE: No, [3]... staying in and watching the football on television?

SUE: Oh no! Come on! [4]... go and see the film!

DAVE: OK, you win. But I'd rather watch the football.

Fact or fantasy?
Bela Lugosi, the most famous Dracula of the cinema, was born in Romania, the traditional home of the vampire.
(Answer on page 111).

21 Haunted House

A

Do you think that ghosts exist? Have you ever been to a haunted place?

B

Look at the diagram. Which of the things that happened do you think was the most frightening? Why do you think the things happened?

Living Room		Study
Door	Hall	
Dining Room The family were having lunch when they saw the figure of a woman outside, asking for food.	**Kitchen** Mrs Johnson was making the supper one night when somebody threw a wine bottle at her.	
Bathroom Sarah was having a bath when some writing appeared on the wall.	**Mr and Mrs Johnson's bedroom**	
Andrew's Bedroom Andrew was playing in his room when he saw a little girl in the garden wearing old-fashioned clothes.	**Sarah's Bedroom** Sarah was reading in bed when she heard terrible screams	

C

Read the diary and find out the cause of the hauntings. Then use the diagram to complete the diary.

Example: 1 = playing

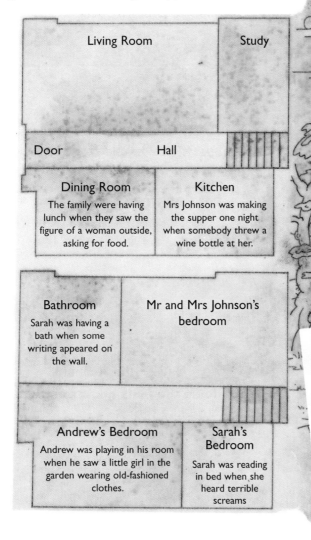

19th September
We moved into our new house today. It's got a fantastic garden.

22nd September
Somebody at school said our new house is haunted. I don't believe in ghosts!

6th October
Andrew was ¹___ in his room this afternoon when he saw a little girl in the garden. The girl was ²___ old-fashioned clothes. I think Andrew is seeing things!

31st October
Halloween! I was ³___ a bath tonight when some writing suddenly appeared on the wall. It said 'GET OUT'. I looked at the writing and it was in blood! I am getting scared!

18th November
We were in the dining room and we were ⁴___ lunch, when we saw the figure of a woman outside. She was ⁵___ for food and looking at our plates. This is not funny any more!

Language Focus: Past continuous/past simple

D

Look at these sentences from the diary. Put them in order of when they happened.

a   I looked at the writing.
b   I was having a bath.
c   Writing suddenly appeared on the wall.

Which tense is used to describe:

- an activity (what I was doing)?
- an action (what happened)?
- a reaction (what happened after that)?

> 5th December
> Mum was ⁶___ supper in the kitchen when somebody threw a wine bottle at her. She says there was nobody else in the kitchen. She wants to leave the house.
>
> 25th December
> Last night was horrible! It was very late and I couldn't sleep. I was ⁷___ in bed when I heard terrible screams and all the windows smashed. Somehow we all got out of the house. Outside everything was quiet. We are never going into that house again and we have decided to sell it.
>
> 6th January
> I went to the local library today. I found out that the house had been the old poorhouse. It closed in 1892, after the director had gone mad and murdered several of the poor people. The murders happened on the 24th of December !!!

E

Copy and complete these tables for the past continuous.

AFFIRMATIVE

I/He/She/It	....	having	lunch.
You/We/They	....	....	a book.

NEGATIVE

I/He/She/It	....		
You/We/They	....	not	having a shower.

QUESTIONS

What	....	I/he/she/it	doing?
	....	you/we/they	

F

Write five negative sentences about the story.

Example: Sarah wasn't sleeping when she heard the screams.

G

Imagine that you lived in the haunted house. Invent five things that happened when you were there.

Example: I was listening to music in my room when I saw a horrible face at the window.

H

In pairs, interview your partner, like this:

Action   A: What happened?
Activity A: What were you doing when it happened?
Reaction A: What did you do?

MIRACULOUS SURVIVORS

British explorer, Sir Ernest Shackleton, wanted to walk across Antarctica. He left England with thirty men in the ship *Endurance* in July 1914. *Endurance* reached South Georgia in September 1914 and after three weeks it left again. Then it disappeared. No one knew what had happened to it.

While *Endurance* was sailing across the Weddell Sea at the beginning of 1915, the weather got colder. The ship became trapped by ice inside a frozen sea of a million square kilometres. For six months they could not escape from the ship. Then, in October, *Endurance* began to break up. The crew had enough time to take food and equipment off the ship before it sank on 21 November. The men were now no longer in a warm, safe and comfortable ship. They were now living a cold, wet, and dangerous life on the ice.

Shackleton thought they should wait where they were until the ice carried them nearer to land. While they were moving slowly north, 1916 arrived but they still hadn't reached land. They finished their sugar and bread and they had to kill birds and animals for food. Later they also shot their horses. In March 1916 the ice began to break up and they saw land at last.

On April 5 they got into the three lifeboats. Unfortunately the sea and wind carried them into open water away from the land. They were in freezing boats for a week before they could land at a place called Elephant Island. The island was uninhabited and they could not stay there but the men were not strong enough to go on after six months on the ice.

Shackleton decided to sail with the four strongest men to South Georgia, the place from where *Endurance* had left nearly eighteen months before. Shackleton and the men left on 24 April and reached South Georgia on 10 May, after a terrible journey of over a hundred kilometres in an open boat through stormy seas and freezing weather. And they still had to climb over a mountain of 1,500 metres and walk across the island to get to the whaling factory!

At two in the afternoon on May 20th the manager was very surprised to see men with thin faces and long hair walking across the snow to his factory. "Who are you?" he asked, although he had met Shackleton before. "We have met before," was the reply. Then Shackleton told the manager about the other men. Later a whaling ship went to Elephant Island to collect the rest of the group.

Shackleton had not crossed Antarctica but he had brought out all the men alive from the coldest and most dangerous place in the world.

A

Have you ever heard a story you did not believe, but later you found out it was true? Tell the class.

Example: My uncle said he saw a firewalker in India- it is true (he's got the photos).

B

Read the text about Ernest Shackleton again. Do you believe the story? Why? Why not?

C

Read it again and put it these events in order:

Example: c = 1

a ... the wind and the sea carried the sailors away from the land
b ... a ship collected the other sailors from Elephant Island
c ... *Endurance* left South Georgia
d ... the sailors were moving slowly north on the ice, 1916 arrived
e ... Shackleton told the manager about the other men
f ... *Endurance* sank

D KEYWORDS

Fill in the gaps in exercise C with the words and expressions below.

Example: **a** *Unfortunately* the wind and the sea carried the sailors away from the land

| while on 21 November unfortunately |
| after three weeks then later |

E

Now listen to the correct version of the story. How many mistakes can you find in the story?

Example: 1 *Endurance* left with Shackleton and 27 men, not 30 men.

F

Think of a real situation (or invent a false one) where you were in danger but escaped.

Write notes like these:

When and where did it happen?
in 1986 – on a farm with my parents
What were you doing when it happened?
playing near a pond
What happened?
fell into pond – couldn't swim
How did you escape?
farmer heard me – pulled me out
How did you feel afterwards?
frightened – never played near a pond / afraid of water

G

In groups, tell your stories (using the expressions from exercise D). Decide which stories are true. Choose one story to tell the rest of the class.

Example: In 1986 I was with my parents on a farm. I was playing near a pond, when suddenly ...

H DICTIONARY SKILLS

Use the mini-dictionary to correct the spelling of these words. Then classify the words as noun, verb, adjective or adverb.

1 rughly
2 wordwide
3 volanteer
4 manufacturd
5 kindom
6 iestablish
7 selfdefence
8 unconscous
9 mairaculously
10 cosmanauts

23 Fluency

A 🔊

Listen to the descriptions. Who or what are they describing?

B 🔊

Listen again. Which of the creatures:

a have sharp teeth? *Werewolf* ✓
b haunt old buildings? *Ghost* ✓
c wear old-fashioned *Dracula* ✓
   clothes?
d have a large head? *Frankenstein*
   monster ✓

C 📖

Read the horror story and match these titles with the paragraphs.

· escape from the Slothar
· a strange dream
· a mysterious house
· meeting the Hypnoth

D 🔑 KEYWORDS

Which of these adjectives from the text describe:

a something negative?
b size?

> horrible enormous terrible
> tall sinister large small big

THE SUNDAY HERALD
HORROR STORY
COMPETITION

THE LOCH MORAR MONSTERS by Angela Tranter

1 Last year I was with my family on holiday in Scotland. We were staying in a house on Loch Morar. On the first night I had a horrible dream. I dreamt about a cave where a scientist was doing terrible experiments. He was experimenting on animals and people and creating strange creatures. There was a very strong monster called the Slothar and another called the Hypnoth that hypnotised people.

2 I woke up in the morning and forgot about my dream. That afternoon I was walking with my brother along the loch. We came to a house with a wild garden. On the wall was a large notice which said "LOCH MORAR LABORATORY — — KEEP OUT". This was the place from my dream! We climbed over the wall and saw the entrance to a cave.

3 We went in and walked along a dark passage. Suddenly, we saw an enormous creature, nearly three metres tall. It had a sinister, square head covered with thin hair. Its eyes were small, but it had a large mouth with horrible, pointed teeth. At the end of its long arms were two sharp claws. It moved quickly towards us. I took out my torch and shone it into the Slothar's eyes so it couldn't see. Then we ran down the passage.

4 After that, we saw the figure of a small, old man. He was less than a metre tall and had very thin legs and arms. His head was too big for his body and he had two bright blue eyes. He was wearing old-fashioned clothes.
He looked at us for a long time. He was hypnotising us ...

Final Writing Task: A story

Imagine that you are the person in the story. Write an ending.

Stage 1 Use the diagram to make notes.

Example: took out sword / killed Hypnoth / across a river, etc.

> **WHAT HAPPENED NEXT**
> how you escaped from the Hypnoth
> where you went

> **WHAT HAPPENED AFTER THAT**
> what you saw
> what your reaction was

> **WHAT HAPPENED IN THE END**
> how you escaped
> how you felt

Stage 2 Write the ending to the story. Try to use some of these words.

> after that / then / when / while / suddenly / later / in the end

Stage 3 Give your ending to your partner to read and to look for mistakes. Then write a final version.

Final Speaking Task: A Story

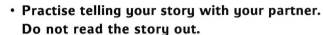

- **Practise telling your story with your partner. Do not read the story out.**
- **Use your notes and the expressions from stage 2 to help you.**
- **In groups, tell your story to the others. Decide which is the most interesting ending in your group. Report it to the rest of the class.**

Listen to another ending to the story. Answer these questions:

1 How did they escape from the Hypnoth?
  a running **b** with a mirror **c** with a sword
2 What did they find in the laboratory?
  a some children **b** more monsters
  c dead people
3 Who put them in the cage?
  a the Hypnoth **b** Dr Clawstein **c** the Slothar
4 Who opened the cage door?
  a the children **b** the Slothar **c** his brother
5 What did the computer destroy?
  a the monsters **b** the children **c** the cage
6 What happened to Dr. Clawstein?
  a he died **b** he escaped
  c the police arrested him
7 Why did their parents call the police?
  a they got a telepathic message
  b they saw a monster **c** they heard noises

Which ending do you prefer, this one or yours?

24 Consolidation

Grammar

A

Read the story of *The Black Cat of Killakee*. Do you believe it? Put the verbs in brackets into the past simple or past continuous.

Killakee House is a large old house near Dublin in Ireland. In 1968, when Mrs O'Brian moved in, the villagers [1]... (tell) her it was haunted. Then, one night in March, Mrs O'Brian was with some friends in the house. They [2]... (paint) the hall of the house, when the door [3]... (open). They [4]... (see) a figure outside. It [5]... (wear) black clothes and [6]... (stand) in the garden but they [7]... (not see) its face.

B

Correct the mistakes in the second part of the story.

The misterius figure said at her: "Leave this door open!" When Mrs O'Brian heared that, she closed the front door and runned towards the door kitchen. When she get there she looked back. The door was open and there was an cat enormous black in the hall. The cat was sat there and looking to her with horible large red eyes.

C

Complete the poem below with past participles.

Have you ever [1]...
lunch with a vampire?
Have you ever [2]...
across a very hot fire?
Have you ever [3]...
a ghost in the lavatory?
Have you ever [4]...
to a monster laboratory?
I haven't and I don't think I'd like to!

Vocabulary

D   KEYWORDS

Match the adjectives with their opposites.

Example: 1 very small / enormous

> thin / old-fashioned / east / soft / poor /
> small / dark / common / strange / long /
> unconscious / enormous

1 very small	**5** thick	**9** conscious
2 short	**6** modern	**10** bright
3 normal	**7** hard	**11** rich
4 uncommon	**8** big	**12** west

E

Complete the story with these verbs.

get out / look back / take out / turn into /
find out / keep out

It was 10 o'clock at night and there was a full moon when I [1]... that my French teacher was a werewolf. I was walking near the school when I heard a strange noise coming from the language laboratory. I [2]... my torch and walked towards the building. A notice on the door said [3] "...", but I entered the room. My teacher was there. Suddenly, he [4]... a werewolf with enormous teeth and ears. I [5]... of the room very quickly and ran. I did not [6]...!

VOCABULARY GAME

F

In groups, choose a letter. Individually, think of as many words starting with the letter as you can. Do not look in the book or your vocabulary book!
Then play the game. If you cannot say a word immediately, you are out. You can't repeat words!

Example: letter 'b': A: big
                                    B: bathroom
                                    C: bus
                                    D: er ... well ... (out of game)

Pronunciation

G

Listen to some of the different ways that you can pronounce the letter 'e'.

Group 1	Group 2	Group 3	Group 4
/e/ ever	/ə/ later	/iː/ he	/ / walked (no sound)

Listen to these words and put them in the correct group. Can you find more words from this module to put into each group?

extra / other / bend / disaster / we / bigger / crossed / garden / smallest / she / bedroom / longer

Test Yourself

A (8 points)

Put the verbs in brackets in the present perfect or past simple.

Many people ¹... (have) psychic experiences about the past and some people ²... (see) people from the past in historic places. For example, in 1960 a man ³... (see) a group of vikings land and attack the Scottish island of Iona. These attacks really ⁴... (happen) in the ninth century. Other people ⁵... (imagine) previous lives. One man said he ⁶... (be) a soldier in the Roman

army in 55 B.C. Under hypnosis he ⁷... (describe) ancient Rome and ⁸... (understand) Latin perfectly.

B (7 points)

Put the verbs in brackets in past simple or past continuous.

In 1901 two English teachers ¹... (visit) the palace of Versailles in France when something strange happened. They ²... (walk) in the gardens when suddenly they ³... (hear) music and ⁴... (see) people from the eighteenth century. These people ⁵... (wear) old-fashioned clothes and they ⁶... (sing) old songs. That day there ⁷... (be) no play at the theatre or anything else to explain it.

Extra Time

Look at Reading Club 4 on page 98.

Module Check

PRESENT PERFECT
Affirmative
Many people **have walked** across fires without burns.
Negative
I **haven't** ever **seen** a ghost.
I **have** never **seen** a ghost.
Questions
Have you ever **had** a premonition?

PRESENT PERFECT/PAST SIMPLE
Have you **seen** that film? Yes, I **have**. (short answer) I **saw** it last year. (specific time in the past)

PAST CONTINUOUS
Affirmative
I **was reading** in bed when I heard terrible screams.
Negative
She **was not listening** when Sarah spoke.
Questions
What **were** you **doing** when you saw the face?

- Make sure you know the meaning of these words and expressions.
- Put important new words in your vocabulary book.

Horror: werewolf, vampire, ghost, monster
Films: science fiction, horror, adventure
Houses: bedroom, bathroom, kitchen, study
Physical description: square head, pointed teeth, blue eyes, sharp claws, old-fashioned clothes
Adjectives with similar meaning: curious/mysterious, huge/enormous, brilliant/fantastic, amazing/incredible, sinister/strange, frightened/afraid
Adjectives with opposite meaning: soft/hard, bright/dark, short/long (tall), big/small, modern/old-fashioned, west/east, thick/thin
Invitations and suggestions: Would you like to come and see Alien? Let's go and see E.T. How about meeting at 8 o'clock?
Verbs: move, lift, bend, touch, dream, breathe, get out, look back, take out, turn into, find out, keep out
- **Try to add more words to each list.**

Module diary

- **Which was your favourite lesson in module 4? Why?**

  Example: Haunted House - because I like ghosts.

- **Which of these things do you believe in now?**
  levitation / telepathy / firewalking / ghosts

- **Which reading text did you like most? Which was the most difficult?**
  - the article about Special Powers
  - the diary of the haunted house
  - the story about Shackleton and the Antarctic
  - the story about the monsters

- **Which of these things did you do, when you wrote your ending to the story?**
  - used the diagram to generate ideas
  - organised paragraph notes
  - got your partner to check when you have finished
  - wrote a final version

- **What was your score in the *Test Yourself*?**

- **Give yourself a mark for these structures.**
  - Present perfect/past simple   • Past continuous
  A I understand it very well.
  B I sometimes make mistakes.
  C I don't understand it.

- **Give yourself a mark from 1-10 for these things:**
  - Participation in class   • Interest/effort
  - Homework

SPORT

Lead-in

Module Objectives

In this module you will ...

Read a sports questionnaire, a magazine article about Dennis Bergkamp and a TV guide.

Talk about your favourite sports and players.

Listen to a survey and TV sports commentaries.

Practise using conditional type 2 sentences and question tags.

Your **final tasks** will be to **write** and **tell the class** about a sport.

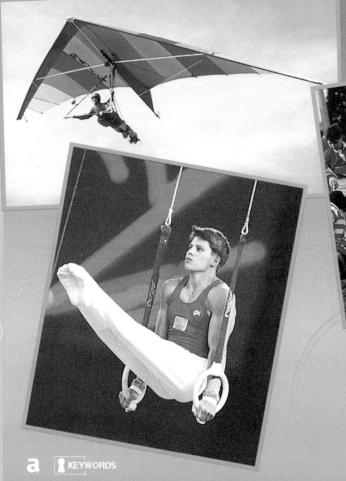

a 🔑 KEYWORDS

Which sports can you see in the photos? In pairs, copy the network below and classify these sports:

parachuting hockey tennis basketball
golf horse riding canoeing climbing
swimming table tennis football skating
skateboarding skiing sailing athletics
judo cycling squash water skiing
volleyball karate

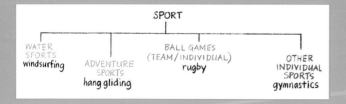

SPORT

WATER SPORTS — windsurfing
ADVENTURE SPORTS — hang gliding
BALL GAMES (TEAM/INDIVIDUAL) — rugby
OTHER INDIVIDUAL SPORTS — gymnastics

b

In pairs, find out which sports your partner:

has played / does regularly / thinks are the most exciting / thinks are really boring / thinks are very dangerous

Example: A: Which sports have you played?
        B: I've played football, basketball and tennis.

ARE YOU A SPORTS FANATIC?

Does the mention of the word 'sport' make you run and put on your trainers? Or look for somewhere to hide? Answer these questions and find out how much you like sport. Be honest!

1 It's a cold, wet Sunday afternoon. Do you:
   a) go out and play a game?
   b) watch sport on TV?
   c) read a book?

2 The World Cup Final is on TV. Do you:
   a) watch the match?
   b) study and listen to the match on the radio?
   c) go to your bedroom and play on your computer?

3 The Olympics are taking place on the other side of the world. Do you:
   a) stay up all night to watch everything?
   b) read the results in the morning newspaper?
   c) yawn when friends talk about it?

...and Russia got the gold medal...

4 Your new boyfriend/girlfriend wants to play tennis on Saturday. Do you:
   a) agree immediately and practise every day?
   b) go, but say you're not very good?
   c) say you're not interested and suggest going to the cinema?

5 The sports teacher is talking to the class about organising a sports day. Do you:
   a) volunteer for every event?
   b) choose one event you'd like to be in?
   c) hide behind a big student?

6 Your sports teacher chooses you to run in the 1500 metres race. Do you:
   a) practise running for a week before the race?
   b) just do your best and not worry about winning?
   c) phone the school on the day and say you are ill?

A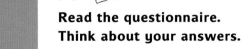

Read the questionnaire. Think about your answers.

B

In pairs, interview your partner and find out his/her score.

C

Listen to Sheila and Alan. Write down their answers to the questionnaire and calculate their points.

Points		Results
a)	5 points	6 points or less: You hate sport.
b)	3 points	7-18 points: You quite like sport.
c)	0 points	More than 18 points: You're a sports fanatic!

Language Focus: Conditional sentences (2)

D

Listen again and match the two parts of the sentences.

Example: 1 = c

1 If it was cold and wet,
2 If England was playing,
3 If the Olympics were on the other side of the world,
4 If she wanted to play tennis,
5 If the sports teacher chose me,

a I'd watch the match.
b I wouldn't practise every day, but I'd go.
c I'd probably stay in and read a book.
d he would be crazy.
e I'd read the results in the morning paper.

E

Look at the sentences in the box. Are the situations real or imaginary? Which of these tenses do we use for the condition and which for the consequence?

• past simple or continuous
• conditional (*would* + verb)

CONDITION	CONSEQUENCE
If the sports teacher chose me,	he would be crazy.
If England was playing,	I'd watch the match.
If the World Cup Final was on TV,	you would go to your bedroom.

F

In pairs, ask about the situations below and give full answers.

Example: A: What would you do if you won two tickets to a basketball final?
B: If I won two tickets to a basketball final, I would sell them!

1 What / do / if / win two tickets to a basketball final?
2 Which sports star / invite to your party / if / have a choice?
3 What sport / play / if / can be a champion?
4 Which new sport / choose / if / your sports teacher ask you?
5 What sport / play / if / not have any homework?

G

PRONUNCIATION

Listen to the sentences and write them down. How many words are in each sentence? Contractions, such as *wouldn't*, count as two words.

Example: If England were playing, I'd watch the match. = 9 words.

Did you know?

Surfing is an ancient Polynesian sport. The first European to see it was Captain Cook when he visited Tahiti in 1771.

Champions

She is the record goal scorer for the USA's women's soccer team.

One of the greatest basketball players of all time.

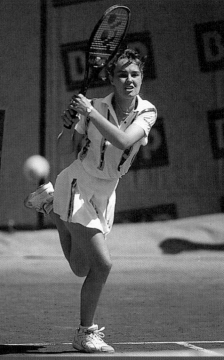

She was a tennis champion at the age of sixteen.

A

Match the names with the photos.

Martina Hingis / Michael Jordan / Michael Johnson / Michelle Akers

B

If you could be a champion, who would it be? Tell the class.

Example: If I could be a champion, I would be Ronaldo.

C

Who are the best teams and players *now*? In pairs, ask your partner.

Examples: Who is the best cyclist?
Which is the best women's volleyball team?

One of the most brilliant athletes ever.

Tell the class one thing about your partner.

Example: Maria thinks Victor is the best footballer.

D

Read about Dennis Bergkamp. Copy and complete the timeline.

```
1 ........           3 ........        4 ........  USA World Cup
  |                    |                 |
1969 —— 1986 —— 1990 —— 1992 —— 1993 —— 1994 —— 1995 —— 1998
        |                        |                 |            |
      2 ........            top scorer in       5 ........  record scorer
                          European Championship             for Holland
```

A Hero from Holland

Dennis Bergkamp has been one of Holland and Europe's most talented footballers in recent years. He was born in 1969 in Amsterdam and grew up there. People noticed very quickly there was something special about him. The
5 football academy of the Ajax Football Club took him on at the age of twelve and in 1986 he made his debut for the Ajax first team when he was just 17 years old. This was the start of Dennis's incredible career.

Dennis scored four goals which helped Ajax to win the
10 European Cup Winners' Cup in 1987. He was top scorer in Holland in 1990 and for the next two years. He was recognised as the best young player in Europe and in 1992 he was voted the Dutch Player of the Year for the second time. Dennis was also the top scorer in the
15 European Championship in Denmark that same year.

In 1993 Dennis left Ajax and joined the Italian club Inter Milan. While he was playing with Inter, Dennis was a member of the Dutch team which reached the semi-finals at the World Cup in the USA in 1994. While in the USA he decided not to fly again and since then he has always travelled to matches by car, train or boat, never by plane.

20 Dennis did not like the defensive style of Italian football so he moved to the English club Arsenal in 1995 for $12,000,000. He became very successful and in May 1998 helped Arsenal to win both the FA Cup and Premier League championship. In July of the same year he was in the Dutch team to play in the World Cup in France. He scored a superb goal as Holland beat Argentina 2-1 in the quarter final. With this goal
25 Dennis Bergkamp became the record scorer for his country.

E

Now answer these questions.

1 Where did Dennis Bergkamp grow up?
2 In which year was Dennis the top scorer in the European Championship?
3 In which year did Dennis stop travelling by plane?
4 Why did Dennis leave Inter Milan?

F KEYWORDS

What are the correct definitions of these words in this context?

1 grew up (line 3)
   a got taller   b got older
2 took him on (line 5)
   a started a fight
   b gave him a place
3 made his debut (line 6)
   a started his training
   b played for the first time
4 he was recognised as (line 11)
   a people knew what he looked like   b people thought of him as

G KEYWORDS

Find five words in the text that mean "very good".

Example: talented

Are the words similar in your language?

H

GUESS THE CHAMPION

In groups, take turns to say a sentence about a player or team. The others guess who it is.

Examples: She won the women's singles at Wimbledon last year.

27 Wacky Sports

A

Look at the photos and read the captions. Which 'wacky' sport would you like to try?

BAR FLY FLYING: Jump from a trampoline and stick yourself to a velcro-covered wall!

BUNGEE JUMPING: Jump from a high place on an elastic cable!

SNOWBOARDING: All the excitement of surfing — on snow!

CRAZY SUMO WRESTLING: fight your opponent with a huge inflated sumo doll!

B

Copy the club membership form. Then listen to the conversation and complete it.

THE WACKY ZONE

MEMBERSHIP APPLICATION FORM

DATE: 2nd September

NAME: Christine Corkhill

ADDRESS: 25, Green Lane, Winchester

DATE OF BIRTH: ....

SPORTS: ....

DO YOU WANT COACHING SESSIONS?

(specify sports): ....

Language Focus: Question tags

C

Listen again and write each sentence with the correct question tag.

Example: Your full name is Christine Corkhill, isn't it?

SENTENCE	QUESTION TAG
Your full name **is** Christine Corkhill,	**are** you?
You **aren't** Colin's sister,	**do** you?
He **won**,	**isn't** it?
You **don't live** near here,	**don't** you?
You**'re** under sixteen,	**didn't** he?
You **want** to do bungee jumping and snowboarding,	**aren't** you?

Now copy and complete the rule.

In a negative sentence the question tag is ...
In an affirmative sentence the question tag is ...

D

Complete these sentences with suitable question tags.

1 She likes windsurfing, ...? *doesn't she*
2 He's good at tennis, ...? *isn't he*
3 They didn't play very well, ...? *did they*
4 He can't swim, ...? *can he*
5 You were in the school team, ...? *weren't you*
6 He hasn't played squash before, ...? *has he*

E

PRONUNCIATION
Listen to the questions. In which of them is the person unsure of the answer?

Example: number 2
Listen and repeat.

F

In pairs, imagine you are applying to join a sports club. Copy the application form in exercise B again and complete it for yourself. Give the form to your partner. He/she checks it, like this:

Example: A: Your name is ... , isn't it?
B: Yes, it is.

G

QUESTION TAG GAME

In pairs, student A makes a statement. students B adds the question tag.

A: You don't like football ...
B: ... do you?
B: Last week she joined the club ...
C: ... didn't she?

H

Use the mini-dictionary to choose the correct form of the word.

1 The soldier was famous because of his brave / bravery.
2 Don't touch that snake! Its bite can be deadly / death.
3 There were three survived / survivors from the car crash.
4 There has been a lot of develop / development here in the last ten years.
5 Exercise is very important to help you stay health / healthy.
6 Be careful with your money. I don't want you to lose / lost it.
7 Jane heard noises / noisy in the kitchen and phoned the police.
8 Damian spent his child / childhood in a large house in the country.

TV GUIDE

BBC1

2.00 **The Clothes Show:** Teenagers talk about buying clothes

2.30 **Tennis:** The Australian Open. Sabatini v Sánchez Graf v Novotna

5.15 **Cartoons:** Tom and Jerry

6.00 **News**

BBC2

2.30 **Basketball:** NBA games- Detroit Pistons v Boston Celtics

3.15 **Way West** (film 1967): A cowboy film with Kirk Douglas, Robert Micham and Richard Widmark

5.00 **Rugby Special:** Scotland v Wales / Ireland v France

6.00 **Ski Sunday:** The World Championships from Val d'Isère, France

Channel 4

2.00 **The Winslow Boy** (film 1948)

4.10 **Czech cartoons**

4.30 **News Summary**

4.40 **Scottish Eye:** 'Fowl Play': poisoning of rare birds in Scotland

4.40 **The Waltons:** The Silver Wings

ITV

2.00 **Charlie's Angels** (repeat): Guest stars Kate Jackson and Cheryl Ladd

2.55 **The Match:** Manchester Utd v Liverpool. Football from Old Trafford

5.05 **International Athletics:** The Assurance National Indoor Championships from Cosworth

6.35 **Golf:** New Zealand Open from Auckland

A

Do you watch sports programmes on television? Tell the class your favourite.

B

Read the TV guide. Which programmes do you think these people would watch?

1　John - he's learning to play golf.
2　Anne - she likes animals.
3　Emma - she wants to be a top model.
4　David - he likes westerns.

Which two programmes would you like to watch? Tell the class.

C

Look at the times of the programmes. Are the following things *possible* or *impossible*?

1　Mark wants to watch *Rugby Special* and *International Athletics*.
2　Jane wants to watch *Tennis* and *Ski Sunday*.
3　Dennis wants to watch *Way West* and *The Waltons*.

D

Listen to two commentaries. Which of the sporting events in the TV guide are they from?

E KEYWORDS

Listen again. Write down the adverbs from the box which you hear.

> never slowly happily nervously usually
> occasionally hard quickly fast suddenly
> desperately often nearly angrily calmly
> bravely well clearly noisily beautifully
> completely

F

Complete the text with the adverbs below. Read the whole text before you start!

happily / gradually / never / slowly / nervously / fast / sadly / always

> Before races Manuela ¹... felt nervous. But she had ²... felt like this before. She walked out ³... into the stadium. She waited ⁴... for the race to start. The race started and in the first few metres she saw her American rival running ⁵... in front of her. She began to catch up with her ⁶... . With ten metres to go they were level and Manuela won by a few centimetres. She smiled ⁷... at the crowd as the American walked away ⁸... .

G

ADVERB GAME

> In groups, each student says this sentence: 'What are you doing?'. First decide how you are going to say it.
>
> slowly / nervously / violently / calmly / fast / sadly / happily
>
> **The others say *how* you said the sentence.**
>
> **Play the game again with a new sentence.**

Did you know?

Richard K. Brown in California once skateboarded at 115.53 k/p/h.

A KEYWORDS

Match these words with the numbers in the pictures.

boots skirt helmet skis racket trainers
referee bat pads umpire ball skates
club skateboard net sticks court shorts

B

Read the school magazine article and answer these questions.

1 Why did Elaine start judo classes?
2 Why does she enjoy the club?
3 Why is the colour of the belt important?
4 What is another name for a judo teacher?
5 How often does Elaine have judo classes?

MY SPORT: JUDO BY ELAINE TAYLOR

"Me doing Judo"

I started at a judo club near my house a year ago. My mother thought it was a good idea for girls to learn self-defence. I enjoy going to the club because I have met a lot of new friends. You don't need any special equipment. You just need to wear loose white trousers and a jacket, called a 'judo-gi'. There are no buttons on the jacket - you tie it with a belt. The colour of the belt is important, because it shows how good you are. The best judo teachers, or 'Dans', wear a black belt. My belt is orange - I'm getting quite good. In judo, you fight your opponent on a square carpet, 10 metres x 10 metres. You get points for lifting, throwing and holding your opponent. I go to my judo club every Tuesday and Thursday after school and our club plays matches against other clubs. I like watching judo in the Olympics, but I don't think I'll ever be that good.

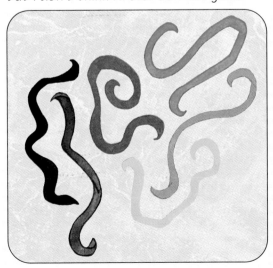

Stage 2 Use your notes to write three paragraphs.

Stage 3 Ask another student to check your work for spelling and punctuation.

Stage 4 Write your article neatly. Include photos, drawings and tables if you wish.

Final Speaking Task: My sport

D

Tell the class or your group about your favourite sport.

- Look at the notes you wrote in exercise C. Do not read out your article.

- In pairs, practise talking about your sport to your partner. If you find some parts difficult, think about what to leave out.

- Give your talk to the class. If you have prepared your talk at home, you can bring things in (e.g. equipment, medals, photos) to show the class.

Final Writing Task: My sport

C

Sports project

Write an article about your favourite sport for the school magazine.

Stage 1 Write some **notes** about these things.

- When and why you became interested in the sport.
- What equipment and clothes you need to do it.
- Things you do:
  - play the sport (how often? where? who with?).
  - watch it (on TV, go to matches,).
  - collect things (photos, magazines, stickers, badges?).

Did you know?
Martina Navratilova played seventy four consecutive tennis matches without losing.

30 Consolidation

Grammar

A

Put the verbs in brackets in the correct tense for these imaginary situations.

Example: If he didn't argue with the referee, he wouldn't get so many yellow cards.

1 If he ..... (not argue) with the referee, he ..... (not get) so many yellow cards.
2 I ..... (buy) some new trainers if I ..... (have) enough money.
3 If you ..... (be) a professional footballer, what team ..... you ..... (like) to play for?
4 If he ..... (not smoke), he ..... (be) healthier.
5 They ..... (lose) more often if they ..... (not have) a good goalkeeper.

B

In groups, one student thinks of an imaginary situation and tells the group. The others add more sentences, like this:

A: If I won the lottery, I would buy a <u>motorbike</u>.
B: If I bought a <u>motorbike</u>, I would go to the <u>coast</u>.
C: If I went to the <u>coast</u>, I would ...

See how long you can continue.

C

Add suitable question tags to these sentences.

Example: Stefi plays tennis really well, doesn't she?

1 Stefi plays tennis really well, ... ?
2 Carl Lewis was really fast, ...?
3 She practises every day, ...?
4 I don't have to play, ...?
5 They haven't been to a match before, ...?
6 Pele scored over a thousand goals, ...?

D

In pairs, check what you know about your partner. Ask five questions.

Example: You've got two brothers, haven't you?

Vocabulary

E KEYWORDS

Make adverbs from these adjectives.

> slow happy hard angry good brave
> beautiful fast

F KEYWORDS

Look at these sentences.

1 You *go* swimming.
2 You *play* football.
3 You *do* athletics.

Which verb do we use for:

a ball games?
b most sports ending in –*ing*?
c other sports?

Write five sentences about yourself and sport.

G
GUESS THE SPORT

In groups, one person thinks of a sport and the others have to guess which it is. You only have ten *yes/no* questions.

Example: Is it a team game?

Do you do exercises?
Do you use a ball?
Is it an indoor sport?
Is it an Olympic Sport?

H

Put these verbs into the text in the correct form.

come back / go out / find out / grow up /
go on / look for / take on

GEORGE BEST ¹ ... in
a poor area of Belfast. He
used to ² ... and play football
in the street. Top teams are
always ³ ... young players,
and one day when George
was playing for a local team,
he ⁴ ... that Manchester United
were interested in him. He
went to Manchester for a trial.
He ⁵ ... to Belfast with the good news that the club
wanted to ⁶ ... him ... . It was a good decision. George
Best ⁷ ... to play over 700 games for United and
helped them win the European Cup.

Pronunciation

I

**Listen to the different ways you can pronounce
the letter 'a'.**

Group 1 /eɪ/   take
Group 2 /æ/   match
Group 3 /ɔː/   call

**Now listen and put these words into the
correct group.**

football / athletics / skates /
water / play / walk / race / fall / champion /
almost / famous / game

Example: football = 3

Test Yourself

A   (15 points)

**Read the conversation between the manager
and president of a football club. Put the verbs
in the correct tense to make conditional 2
sentences and add question tags.**

President: Next year is going to be difficult, ¹...?
Manager: Yes. If I ² ... (can), I ³ ... (like) to
buy some new players.
President: The problem is, we're a small club
and we haven't got a lot of money,
⁴ ... ?
Manager: I know. But if you ⁵ ... (give) me
just a few million pounds, we ⁶ ...
(not lose) so many matches, and then
we'd be a bigger club, ⁷ ... ?
President: But money doesn't buy success, ⁸ ... ?
Manager: No, but it helps, ⁹ ... ? If we ¹⁰ ...
(have) two or three new players, we
¹¹ ... (finish) in a good position.
President: You can't be sure, ¹² ...?
Manager: No, but if we ¹³ ... (do), we ¹⁴ ...
(make) more money and you ¹⁵ ...
(get) your money back.
President: I'll see what I can do.

Extra Time

Look at Reading Club 5 on page 99.

Module Check

Language Check

CONDITIONAL TYPE 2

What **would** you **do** if the World Cup Final **was** on TV?

If the World Cup Final **was** on TV, I **would watch** it.

What **would** you **do** if you **didn't have** a lot of homework?

If I **didn't have** a lot of homework, **I'd go out**.

QUESTION TAGS

He **likes** rugby, **doesn't** he?

She **doesn't like** football, **does** she?

They **played** well, **didn't** they?

You **didn't see** the match, **did** you?

He **was** in the team, **wasn't** he?

They **weren't** very lucky, **were** they?

You **haven't played** squash before, **have** you?

She **can't** swim, **can** she?

Keyword Check

- **Make sure you know the meaning of these words and expressions.**
- **Put important new words in your vocabulary book.**

General: score, match, court, record, referee, champion

Clothes and equipment: boots, trainers, shorts, racket, helmet, bat, club, skates, skateboard, sticks, skis

Sports players: tennis player, cyclist, fooballer, swimmer, windsurfer

Sports: volleyball, rugby, tennis, athletics

Playing sports: go (swimming, windsurfing, horse riding, skating), play (football, hockey, rugby, tennis, basketball), do (athletics, karate, judo),

Verbs: grow up, take on, come back, look for, find out

Adjectives/Adverbs: slow/slowly, hard/hard, angry/angrily, fast/fast, beautiful/beautifully

Checking and confirming information: You go to judo classes, don't you?

- **Try to add more words to each list.**

Module diary

- **Which was your favourite lesson in module 5? Why?**

  Example: Lesson 26, Champions, because I like football.

- **Write down something interesting or unusual from the module.**

  Example: Martina Hingis was a champion at the age of sixteen.

- **Look at the reading exercises in Lesson 26. Which of these things did you do?**
  - ignore words because they weren't important
  - guess the meaning of words
  - work out the meaning from the context
  - use a dictionary

- **Give yourself a mark for how well you can do these things in English:**

  - talk about the sports you do or watch
  - talk about sports stars

  A I have some problems but I can communicate.

  B I have a lot of problems but I try.

  C I don't try to talk about them in English.

- **What was your score in the Test Yourself?**
- **Give yourself a mark for:**
  - Conditionals (type 2)
  - Question tags

  A I can do them very well.

  B I sometimes have problems.

  C I don't understand them.

- **How many names of sports can you remember in English?**

- **What are the five most important words you have learnt in this module?**

78

SPACE

Lead-in

Module Objectives
In this module you will ...

Read about the solar system, life in a space colony and cosmonaut training.

Talk about the future, space travel and routines.

Listen to a song, a radio programme and interviews.

Practise making predictions and using present tense passives.

Your **final tasks** will be to **write** a horoscope and **talk** about astronauts.

a 🔑 KEYWORDS

Which of the things in *italics* can you see in the photos?

Our *galaxy*, the Milky Way, contains over 200 billion *stars*!

There are nine planets in our *solar system*.

The *planet* Mars has got two *moons*.

Two Russian *cosmonauts* stayed on the MIR *space station* for over a year.

A *spacesuit* has up to fifteen layers of material to insulate and protect the *astronaut*.

b 📖

Read the sentences in the box and decide if they are true or false. Check your answers on page 111.

c 💬

Would you like to go into space? Tell the class why or why not.

Example: I'd like to go into space because it would be great to look down at the world.

A

Match the pictures with the captions below.

- Meet aliens
- Use suspended animation
- Travel at the speed of light
- Build a space colony
- Land on another planet

B

In groups, discuss which things are possible now. Which do you think we will do in the future? Tell the class.

Examples: We think we will meet aliens.
We think we can land on another planet now.

C 📼

Listen to Dr Edith Lanfear, a scientist, talking about ideas in science-fiction. In what order does she mention the ideas in exercise A?

Language Focus: Talking about predictions

D

Listen again. Look at this extract and complete Dr Lanfear's answers with the words below.

will / may / might / won't

INTERVIEWER: Do you think we will ever meet aliens?
DR LANFEAR: Well, there's a possibility. We [1]... meet some one day.
INTERVIEWER: Do you think we will ever land on another planet?
DR LANFEAR: Yes, we certainly [2]... .
INTERVIEWER: Do you think we will ever build space colonies?
DR LANFEAR: Oh yes. I'm sure we [3]... one day. Scientists from Nasa have already designed one.
INTERVIEWER: Do you think we will ever travel at the speed of light?
DR LANFEAR: No, we [4]... . It's quite impossible.
INTERVIEWER: Do you think we will ever use suspended animation?
DR LANFEAR: Well, we have made some progress with this idea. We [5]... one day.

E

Look at the box and answer the questions.

PREDICTIONS
NO ──────────────➤ YES
won't ──➤ might ──➤ may ──➤ will

1 Which words show that something is:
   a certain
   b impossible
   c possible
2 Which word expresses a less certain possibility, *may* or *might*?

F

Use the ideas below and write sentences about what you think will happen in your lifetime.

Example: We may build colonies in space.

· build colonies in space
· play sports in space
· have a war with aliens
· go on holidays in space
· open mines on the Moon
· go to school in space
· grow food in space

Add another sentence of your own.

G

In pairs, take turns to ask questions about the future.

Example: A: Do you think we will go to school in space?
          B: Well, we might one day.

H

DICTIONARY SKILLS

Use the mini-dictionary to complete the table about these adjectives. If there is no information, the adjective is regular.

ADJECTIVE	COMPARATIVE	SUPERLATIVE
		cloudiest
	wiser	
desperate		
		maddest
scared		
brave		
		most frightened
	lonelier	

32 Our Solar System

Sun **A** **C** **B** **D** **Asteroids** **E** **F**

A 📖

Match the planets with the letters on the diagram.

G	D	E	C	A	F	B
Pluto	Mars	Jupiter	Earth	Mercury	Saturn	Venus

Now read the text and check your answers.

B 📖

Match each paragraph with the best title.

The Outer Planets   The Universe   The Inner Planets

C ✏️

Answer these questions.

1 What is our galaxy called? *Milky way*
2 How hot is the surface of the Sun? *6000°C*
3 How long is a year on Mercury? *88 days*
4 How hot is it on Venus? *500 °C*
5 When did spacecraft first land on Mars? *1976*
6 Why do some scientists think there used to be life on Mars? *Because there is think frozen ice there*
7 What is special about the moon Europa? *Scientists think there might be water there.*
8 How long is a year on Pluto?
   248 Earth years

1 Have you ever tried to count the stars in the night sky? Nobody knows how many there are. A group of stars is called a galaxy, and there are millions of galaxies in the universe. Our sun is one of the smallest stars on the edge of our galaxy, the Milky Way.

2 Let's imagine a tour of our solar system. We begin our journey from the sun, but of course we could never live there – the temperature on the surface is 6000°C! The first planet we see is Mercury. It is strange because the same side always faces the Sun, so one half of the planet is very hot and the other side is extremely cold. It orbits the Sun once every 88 days. The next planet we see is cloudy Venus, which has an atmosphere of poisonous gases and temperatures of up to 500°C! Our Earth is the next planet we pass on our journey.

82

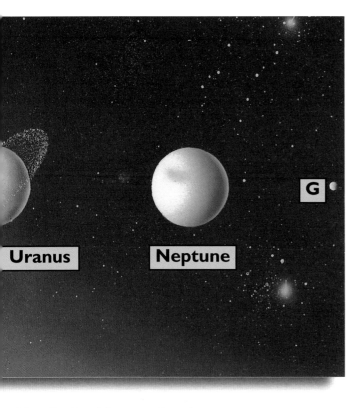

Uranus   Neptune   G

After Earth is Mars, which is the nearest planet to the Earth. Mars is not very warm. Temperatures can fall to -100°C. Spacecraft have landed on Mars a number of times, first in 1976 and more recently in 1997. We now know more about Martian rocks and the Martian atmosphere. Some scientists now believe there used to be primitive life on Mars because there is frozen water there.

3 The next four planets on our tour are giants. The enormous Jupiter has a moon called Europa where scientists think there may also be water. Next is Saturn, famous for its colourful rings of rock and ice which go round it. We know very little about the other two giant planets, Uranus and Neptune, and less about tiny Pluto, the furthest planet from the Sun. Pluto takes 248 Earth years to go round the Sun!

D

Find words in the text which mean the following:

1 One of the large objects like the Earth that go round the Sun. *planet*
2 A mixture of gases that surrounds a planet. *atmosphere*
3 Any of the large groups of stars which make up the universe. *galaxy*
4 Goes round.
  orbit

E

How old are you on Earth and on Mercury?

Example: If you are ten:
  Ten Earth years = 10 x 365 = 3650 days
  One Mercury year = 88 days
  So, 3650 ÷ 88 = 41: You're about 41 Mercury years old!

How old is your mother/sister/teacher on Mercury? Tell the class.

Example: My mother's about 145!

F

Invent a new planet. Copy the table below and fill in the information for your planet.

	MY PLANET
NAME	Ariel
SIZE	very big
MOONS/RINGS	16 moons
DISTANCE FROM SUN	780 million km
LENGTH OF YEAR	11.9 Earth years

In pairs, ask questions to find out about your partner's planet.

Example: What's it called? How big is it?
  How many ...? How far ...?
  How long ...?

A Space Colony

A

Read the description of a space colony. Make notes under these headings:

- transport
- sports
- food
- industry

Example: transport: monorail/rockets

My Space Colony

by Nebula Brown, Class 6C.

20th February, 2050.

I live on Lunar Taurus 12. The colony is like a giant wheel. Rockets arrive and leave from the spaceport in the centre. This is connected by monorails to the wheel where we live. The monorails are very quick and it doesn't take very long to travel anywhere in the colony.

In the spaceport there is a sports centre. I go there twice a week after school. My favourite game is space volleyball. There is no gravity at the centre of the wheel, so you can hit the ball under the net and bounce it off the ceiling!

10,000 people live in our colony on the inside of the wheel. The wheel turns and this creates artificial gravity. Giant mirrors direct sunlight on to the wheel and we have forests, fields and rivers. There's even an artificial beach with a wave-machine, so you can go swimming and surfing.

All our food is grown on the colony. Vegetables are grown on special farms - all the people on the colony are vegetarians. There are also lots of factories. Rockets bring minerals from the Moon and we manufacture everything here from telephones to toothpaste. There's a big factory where rockets are repaired - my father works there.

Nothing on the colony is wasted, of course - everything is recycled. It is incredible to think that fifty years ago on Earth, people destroyed and threw away so many things!

Language Focus: Present simple passive

B

Study the sentences in the box.

> 1 They recycle everything. (Active)
> 2 Everything is recycled. (Passive)
> 3 Rockets bring minerals from the Moon. (Active)
> 4 Minerals are brought from the Moon by rockets. (Passive)

What is the subject in each sentence?

Example: 1 = they

What is the verb?

Example: 1 = recycle

C LEARN TO LEARN

Now answer these questions.

1 The verb in the passive has two parts. What are they?
2 In sentence 2, do we know who recycles everything? Is it important?
3 In sentence 4, do we know what brings minerals from the Moon? Which is more important, the minerals or the rocket?

D

Change these sentences from active to passive.

Example: Artificial gravity is created by the wheel.

1 The wheel creates artificial gravity.
2 Mirrors direct sunlight on to the wheel.
3 They play space volleyball in the sports centre.
4 We manufacture everything here.
5 We grow vegetables on special farms.
6 We repair rockets in the factory.
7 Monorails connect the spaceport with the wheel.

E KEYWORDS

In groups, play this game. You need dice and counters. You have to go round the space colony once and then return to the spaceport. When you land on a square, you have to say a sentence using the passive. If you make a mistake, you miss a turn. When you land on a blank square, do nothing.

Example: A: (*lands on zoo square*) Earth animals are kept here.
B: (*lands on school square*) English are taught here. (*Wrong = miss a turn*)

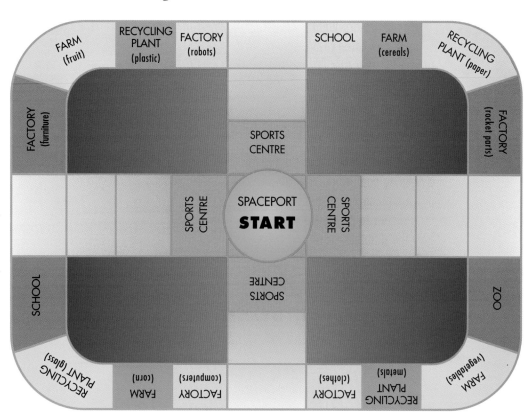

A

Which of these things would you like to do?

- go on holiday in space
- go on a space walk
- live on a space station
- use a space flight simulator

Do you think you will ever have the chance to do any of these things?

B

Which of the things below do you think is the biggest problem for cosmonauts?

- taking off and landing
- eating and drinking
- re-entering the atmosphere
- sleeping

Read the article below and find out.

COSMONAUT FOR A DAY!

Max Dereta investigates Star City, the Russian Space Training Centre in Moscow.

In a few years time, there may be organised holidays to space. But now, if you have the money, you can be a cosmonaut for two days. I decide to go along to Russia's Star City.

First, I go into the simulator of the Soyuz TM space capsule where you can practise space flight. I can't imagine how three cosmonauts can fit into this tiny capsule – and eat, sleep and go to the toilet! The Soyuz TM is used to take cosmonauts to and from the MIR space station.

The next place I visit is the swimming pool, where you can practise doing things in a situation 90% similar to zero gravity. Then I try the simulator of a spacewalker, a rocket-powered " backpack". After about fifteen minutes I get the idea of moving with the backpack. After that I go to the MIR simulator.

This is used to prepare cosmonauts for visits to the MIR space station. The Russians have found that the biggest problem of living in space is returning to gravity again. In the MIR station cosmonauts have to exercise for up to six hours a day to prepare for returning.

Finally, I get the chance to experience weightless conditions. A Russian aeroplane simulates zero gravity perfectly for about 25 seconds at a time. "Get ready," says a voice and suddenly we all rise from the floor, weightless. We float all over the aeroplane, and I take pictures – my heavy cameras weighing nothing. "Twenty-five seconds. Get down."

We repeat this ten times and every second is fantastic. I've still not been to space, but this is the next best thing!

C

Read the article again and answer these questions.

1 What is the Soyuz TM used for?
2 Why are activities done underwater?
3 What is the rocket-powered backpack used for?
4 What is the MIR simulator used for?
5 Where is zero gravity simulated?

D

Are the space facts below true or false? Listen to the radio programme and check your answers.

1 The space race began in the 1960s.
2 The first living creature in space was a Russian dog called Laika.
3 The first man in space was Pavel Belyayvev.
4 The first woman in space was Sally Ride.
5 The first person on the moon was Buzz Aldrin.
6 The Mars Pathfinder, a spaceprobe, landed on Mars in 1997.
7 The Russians hope to send people to Mars in 2020.

E

Invent your own space mission to explore your planet from lesson 32. Write notes like the ones below.

Example:

MISSION ICARUS

date: *2045*
objective: *establish human colony on planet Icarus*
distance from Earth: *6 light years*
predicted journey time: *30 years*
space ship: *Galileo / 270 metres long / 63 astronauts*
life support: *oxygen recycled / food grown on spaceship / suspended animation for long periods*
possible results: *find intelligent life / discover new plants/metals*

F

In pairs, find out about your partner's space mission.

Example: What is your mission called?

· When is your mission going to leave?
· What is the mission going to do?
· How far away is the planet/solar system?
· How long do you think it will take?
· How big is the space ship?
· What kinds of life support will there be?
· What do you think the results will be?

Did you know?

The building where the USA built the Saturn V rocket was so high that clouds formed near the roof!

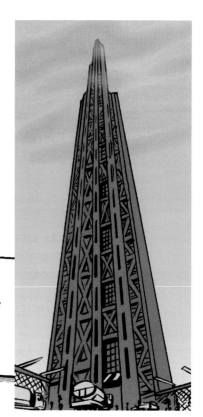

Fluency

A

Read about the four elements *Earth*, *Air*, *Fire* and *Water* and decide which one describes you.

FIRE

Fire is the first of the four signs. People born under fire signs are creative and dynamic. They are also enthusiastic, energetic and show initiative.

WATER

People born under these signs are emotional and passionate. Their feelings dominate them and they often do things without thinking.

AIR

Air is the element of reason. Besides being rational and logical, people born under these signs are often good at organising, analysing or expressing ideas.

EARTH

People born under these signs are the most practical. They also like material things and security.

B

Read the texts again. Find five adjectives that describe personality and write them in your vocabulary book.

Example: creative

C

Which elements do these people belong to?

Example: 1 Paul = Earth

1 Paul is practical. He is good at organising.
2 Robert is dynamic. He has a lot of initiative and energy.
3 Christine is emotional. She often acts without thinking.
4 Sarah is very practical. She likes material things.
5 Charlotte is very logical. She is good at expressing ideas.

Final Speaking Task: A Questionnaire

D

In pairs, ask and answer these questions. Would your partner be a good astronaut? Tell the class why or why not?

ASTRONAUT

◎ Personal information: Age: Height: Weight:
◎ What languages can you speak?
◎ What sports do you do? How often do you do them?
◎ Choose two adjectives to describe your personality: emotional / rational / energetic / practical / dynamic / passionate / creative
◎ What would you do in these situations?

   1   There is a big queue in the shop and people start arguing about who is next. Would you:
       a) go to the front of the queue while the customers are arguing?

E

Look at the stars. Which is your sign of the zodiac?

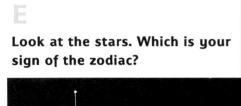

AQUARIUS   SAGITTARIUS   LEO   VIRGO

GEMINI   CAPRICORN

CANCER   ARIES   PISCES   SCORPIO   LIBRA   TAURUS

F

Read this horoscope. Match these words with the predictions:

· love   · family   · money   · friends

1 You will have an argument with your parents early in the week. Don't worry. Things will get better before the weekend.

2 A close friend may ask you for advice about a serious problem. Be honest with them.

3 Someone you have known for a long time might ask you to go out with them. Be positive ~ say yes!

4 Be careful with your money on Friday ~ if you spend too much, you won't have enough for the weekend.

APPLICATION FORM

b) start shouting and arguing with everybody else?

c) try to calm everybody down and find a solution?

d) leave the shop because you're wasting time?

2 You are in a lift with a lot of people when it stops between floors. Would you:

a) panic and start shouting?

b) press the emergency button and wait patiently?

c) tell stories about lift accidents to the other people?

d) try to climb out of the lift?

Final Writing Task: A horoscope

G

Write a horoscope for one sign of the zodiac.

Stage 1
Choose a sign and make notes about:
· family · friends · love · money

Stage 2
Use your notes to write sentences. Use *will/may/might/won't*.

Stage 3
Ask another student to check your sentences for grammar and spelling mistakes.

Stage 4
Write your horoscope neatly. Include a drawing of the zodiac sign.

H

Listen to the song *Rocket Man*. Choose the correct answers.

1 'Zero hour' for the astronaut is: **a** five a.m. **b** nine a.m. **c** 3 p.m.

2 In space he feels: **a** happy **b** angry **c** lonely

3 He is going to: **a** Mars **b** Venus **c** the Moon

4 He doesn't understand: **a** astronomy **b** astrology **c** science

36 Consolidation

Grammar

A

Complete the sentences with these words.

Example: 1 = will

won't / won't / will / will / might / may

1 I'm sure that one day there ... be mines on the Moon.
2 There definitely ... be holidays in space in the next five years.
3 We ... have colonies on Mars in a hundred years time.
4 I think we ... find intelligent life on another planet at some time in the future.
5 We ... ever visit other galaxies, because they are too far away.
6 In the next few years, we ... definitely find out much more about the universe with new telescopes.

B

PREDICTION GAME

In pairs, one person is an optimist and the other a pessimist. If the other person can't reply immediately to your prediction you get one point.

Example: A: I think we will save the Amazon rain forest.
B: I don't. I think we'll destroy it. I don't think we'll ever live on another planet.
A: I do. I think we'll live on Mars. I think we'll ...

C

Change the sentences below.

Example: 1 = Rockets are launched from Cape Canaveral.

1	They launch rockets from Cape Canaveral.	Rockets ...
2	They organise visits to Russia's Star City.	Visits ...
3	Cosmonauts practise zero gravity conditions underwater.	Zero ...
4	They recycle oxygen on space stations with a generator.	Oxygen ...
5	Thick clouds cover Venus.	Venus ...
6	Mercury orbits the Sun every eighty-eight days.	The Sun ...

Vocabulary

D

Complete the sentences below with these words.

gravity station orbits planet galaxies

1 The furthest ... from the Sun is Neptune.
2 There are millions of ... in the universe.
3 Pluto ... the Sun every 248 years.
4 Cosmonauts need to practise living in zero ... conditions.
5 The MIR space ... has been a great success.

E

Make adjectives and adverbs from these nouns.

mystery / beauty / possibility / emotion / energy / logic / enthusiasm / creativity

Example:

NOUN	ADJECTIVE	ADVERB
mystery	*mysterious*	*mysteriously*

F

Complete the sentences with these words.

down / away / over / round / at

1 I am not very good ... organising things.
2 The Earth goes ... the Sun every 365 days.
3 People throw ... a lot of things that could be recycled.
4 After 25 seconds of floating all ... the aeroplane we all got ...

Pronunciation

G

In pairs, look through your vocabulary books and find ten words which are difficult to pronounce. Read out your list to the rest of the class. Which ten words does the class find most difficult to pronounce? Practise saying the words.

H

Look at the words below. Say them. Then listen to the cassette and repeat the words.

1 sky skateboard school score
2 space spaghetti sport speed
3 stretch strange stress strict
4 exercise expert extinct explain

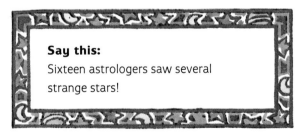

Say this:
Sixteen astrologers saw several strange stars!

Test Yourself

A (8 points)

Complete the alien report about the Earth. Put the verbs in brackets into the passive.

The earthlings are much less advanced than we are. Very basic rockets [1]... (use) to go to space. Their space station is very small and it [2]... (occupy) by only four or five scientists. All the food [3]... (bring) from Earth and nothing [4]... (manufacture) on the space station. Oxygen [5]... (recycle) with a very primitive generator. The planet Earth is in a terrible state. Very few materials [6]... (recycle) and a lot of materials [7]... (waste). The seas and rivers of the planet [8]... (pollute) by factories.

B (7 points)

Complete the sentences with these verbs.

will will / won't won't / may may / might

1 (possible) In the next few years, the earthlings ... build a new space station.
2 (impossible) They ... leave their solar system for a long time.
3 (possible) In the next hundred years they ... establish a space station on Mars.
4 (small possibility) In the future they ... start colonies on other planets.
5 (certain) The earthlings ... destroy the planet Earth, by pollution or nuclear war.
6 (certain) For example, in the next few years, the Earth's climate ... change.
7 (impossible) Humans ... explore all the universe.

Extra Time

Look at Reading Club 6 on page 100.

Language Check

TALKING ABOUT THE FUTURE

Certainty

We **will** definitely establish a colony on the moon in the next fifty years.

Possibility

We **may** use suspended animation in space travel.

Small possibility

We **might** meet aliens one day.

Impossibility

We **won't** ever travel at thespeed of light.

PRESENT PASSIVE

Our food **is grown** in the colony.
Spaceships **are manufactured** by robots.
Everything **is recycled** and nothing **is wasted**.

Keyword Check

- **Make sure you know the meaning of these words.**
- **Put important new words in your vocabulary book.**

Astronomy: planet, galaxy, orbit, universe, solar system, moon, sun

Space flight: space station, rocket, space capsule, zero gravity, oxygen generator

Personality: enthusiastic, dynamic, practical, reserved, rational, emotional, passionate, logical, creative, energetic

Large numbers: three thousand, six hundred and fifty days

Asking questions: how far? / how big? / how long? / how many? / how old?

Plans and predictions: When is your mission going to leave? What do you think the results will be?

- **Try to add more items to the lists.**

Module diary

- **Which was your favourite lesson in module 6? Why?**

  Example: Startrekking. I'd like to be an astronaut.

- **Which of these things could help to improve your pronunciation?**
  - Record and listen to yourself on cassette.
  - Think about the position of your tongue when saying a difficult word.
  - When a word is difficult to pronounce, say another word that means the same. (*Example:* Say *activity* not *exercise*)

- **Look back at your final writing tasks for modules 5 and 6. How can you improve your writing?**
  - planning in more detail
  - taking care not to make mistakes
  - checking your work carefully
  - writing a final version

- **What was your score in the *Test Yourself*?**

- **Give yourself a mark for:**
  - talking about predictions (*will/may/might*)
  - using passives

  A I can do it very well.
  B I sometimes have problems.
  C I don't understand it.

- **How many new words have you learnt from this new module?**

  A more than twenty
  B more than ten
  C less than five

- **Do the End-of-year Self-Assessment on page 111.**

1 – Lesson 1

Ask your partner questions with the cues below. The answers are in brackets.

Example: what / capital / Brazil? (Brasilia)
What is the capital of Brazil?

a where / Manhattan and Brooklyn? (New York)
b where / the Prado museum? (Madrid)
c when / the Olympic Games in Atlanta? (1996)
d where / Big Ben? (London)
e which Andalusian city / Columbus sail from? (Palos de la Frontera)
f which English city / The Beatles from? (Liverpool)
g what / capital / Peru? (Lima)

2 – Lesson 7

Make sentences with the cues below. Your partner says if they are *true* or *false*. The answers are in brackets.

Example: A: Mother Teresa taught geography.
B: True.
A: Correct.

a Mother Teresa / teach / geography. (true)
b Charles Dickens / write / 'Romeo and Juliet'. (false - it was Shakespeare)
c Salvador Dali / paint / 'Guernica'. (false - it was Picasso)
d Christopher Columbus / go / to America in 1492. (true)
e The Rolling Stones / sing / the song 'Yesterday'. (false - it was The Beatles)
f Ricky Martin / make / the record album 'Millennium'. (false - it was Backstreet Boys)
g France / win / the 1998 World Cup. (true)

3 – Lesson 8

Look at the information on this timeline. Follow the instructions in Exercise E and tell your partner the story of William Wallace.

1272 – is born in Scotland
1297 – fights *Battle of Stirling Bridge*, defeats English army
1298 – *Battle of Falkirk*, the English defeat Wallace's army
– escapes to France / later returns to Scotland
1305 – the English capture Wallace in Glasgow / is executed in London

4 – Lesson 11

Read about the Aztecs and make notes. Your partner is going to ask you questions.

The Aztecs built a great empire in Mexico in the 15th century. Their capital, Tenochtitlan, was bigger than any city in Europe at the time. They built it on an island. The Aztecs didn't have transport with wheels. They moved heavy things in boats. Most people ate cereals, and sometimes rabbits or dogs. An omelette cooked with baby frogs was a special meal. The Aztecs discovered how to make rubber balls, and they played a game similar to modern basketball. Their main weapons were spears, clubs, and stones.

5 – Lesson 14

FACTFILE: Gorilla (*gorilla gorilla*)	
Habitat:	forests of equatorial Africa
Size:	MAXIMUM HEIGHT: 1.6 m
	WEIGHT: 181 kg, biggest primates in the world
Physical characteristics:	black hair, small eyes/ears, longer arms than humans but shorter legs
Behaviour:	timid, peaceful, intelligent, good memory, lives in groups of 5-15, lives 30 years
Food:	plants, leaves
Breeding:	similar to humans, young born after 9 months
Population:	in danger of extinction

Pairwork Activities B

1 – Lesson 1

Ask your partner questions with the cues below. The answers are in brackets.

Example: what / capital / Brazil? (Brasilia)
What is the capital of Brazil?

a what / capital / Germany? (Berlin)
b where / the Eiffel Tower? (Paris)
c which Irish city / U2 from? (Dublin)
d where / the Alhambra palace? (Granada)
e when / the Olympic Games in Atlanta? (1996)
f which north American city / called 'The Big Apple'? (New York)
g where / Mother Teresa work? (Calcutta)

2 – Lesson 7

Make sentences with the cues below. Your partner says if they are *true* or *false*. The answers are in brackets.

Example: A: The Ancient Chinese built the Great Wall.
B: False.
A: No, it's true.

a The Ancient Chinese / build / the Great Wall. (true)
b Van Gogh / paint / 'La Giaconda'. (false – it was Leonardo da Vinci)
c Charles Dickens / write / 'Oliver Twist'. (true)
d Neil Armstrong / go / to the moon in 1968. (false – it was 1969)
e Italy / win / the 1990 World Cup. (false - it was Germany)
f Oasis / make / the record album 'Be Here Now'. (true)
g Mariah Carey / sing / the song 'My Heart will Go On'. (false – it was Celine Dion)

3 – Lesson 8

Look at the information on the timeline. Follow the instructions in Exercise E and tell your partner the story of Cleopatra. (Note: B.C. = Before Christ)

69 B.C. – is born in Egypt
51 B.C. – becomes Queen of Egypt
– falls in love with Mark Antony, a Roman
– Mark Antony moves to Egypt
– they fight the Roman army
– Mark Antony thinks Cleopatra is dead and kills himself
30 B.C. – Cleopatra kills herself with a poisonous snake

4 – Lesson 11

Read about the Vikings and make notes. Your partner is going to ask you questions.

The Vikings came from Scandinavia. In the 9th and 10th centuries they travelled to many countries in Europe including Russia, Spain and Turkey. They sailed in long boats and some people think they went to North America. Vikings were violent people and fought with swords and spears. At home, they were farmers. They ate meat and vegetables and drank a type of beer. Vikings enjoyed playing a board game similar to chess, and they also organised horse races.

5 – Lesson 14

FACTFILE: Grey wolf *(canis lupis)*	
Habitat:	plains and forests of Europe, Asia and North America
Size:	LENGTH: 1.6 m WEIGHT: 80 kg
Physical characteristics:	grey fur (sometimes white), strong teeth
Behaviour:	lives in groups (packs), not dangerous to humans
Food:	small animals and birds, sometimes sheep and cows
Breeding:	breeds in spring / similar to dogs – 1 to 11 cubs
Population:	in danger of extinction in western Europe and many parts of North America

A

Read the description of Montevideo. Match these titles with the correct paragraph.

a Great food
b Facts about Montevideo
c Lots to do

Montevideo

1 I live in Montevideo which is the capital of Uruguay. Montevideo is on the Rio de la Plata, opposite Buenos Aires on the other side of the river. It is an attractive city with just over one and a quarter million people. It's a warm and sunny place in the summer and very mild in the winter.

2 I love Montevideo. The people are friendly. The food is cheap and tasty. Parrillada, a beef dish, and chivito, a kind of steak sandwich, are especially delicious. There are lots of great restaurants in Montevideo. If you like sweet things you will love "Martin Fierro", this is a local dessert made of cheese and jam, it tastes fantastic!

3 There are lots of things to do and places to go. You can visit Ciudad Vieja, the old city, close to the harbour, and the Plaza Independencia, a grand square which is home to the Palacio Salvo built in 1927, the tallest building in Montevideo. You can really have fun and excitement during Carnival which takes place in February and March. It's the most exciting time of year to visit Montevideo.

B

Read the text again. In which paragraphs do you find information about theses things? Copy and complete the table.

• location   • weather
• restaurants   • food
• places to go   • population
• when to visit

DESCRIPTION OF MONTEVIDEO: PLAN
Paragraph 1: *location*
Paragraph 2:
Paragraph 3:

C

Are these sentences true or false?

1 Buenos Aires is on the opposite side of Rio de la Plata to Montevideo.
2 Food is very tasty in Montevideo.
3 Ciudad Vieja is a modern area of Montevideo.
4 Chivito is a kind of beef dish.
5 Palacio Salvo is the tallest building in Montevideo.
6 The best time of year to visit Montevideo is in February or March.

A

Read the text and put the paragraphs in the correct order.

Paragraph A ☐   Paragraph B ☐   Paragraph C ☐   Paragraph D ☐

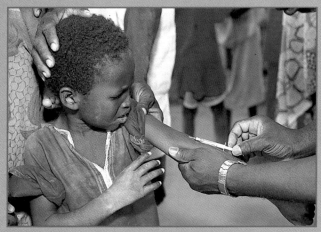

THE STORY OF SMALLPOX

A By the 18th century, there was a form of protection against smallpox. In 1717, Mary Montagu, the wife of a British diplomat in Greece, noticed that village women gave blood from a person with smallpox to healthy people. She brought the treatment to London and it helped to protect people from smallpox. Sadly, some healthy people still caught the disease.

B In 1967, the World Health Organisation started a programme to vaccinate people around the world against smallpox. The programme was expensive and continued for more than ten years. But in the end doctors and scientists won the battle. The disease which used to kill so many people was itself dead. Since 1980 no one has caught smallpox.

C Science and technology have helped us to understand, treat and prevent disease. An example is the story of smallpox. For hundreds of years, smallpox used to kill thousands of people because there was no way to stop the disease.

D A doctor in Britain, Edward Jenner, invented a better treatment in 1796. During his visits to farms Jenner used to talk to dairy maids; country women who worked with cows. They told him that dairy maids who caught cowpox, a disease from cows, never used to catch smallpox, which is much more dangerous than cowpox. He had an idea. He gave a dairy maid with cowpox an injection of smallpox. The dairy maid did not catch smallpox. Jenner had invented vaccinations. With vaccinations, doctors can give people a safe variety of a disease to protect them from the dangerous variety.

B

Read the text again. Copy and complete the table.

WORD	MEANING
1 _____	*a disease which used to kill thousands of people*
dairy maids	2 _____
cowpox	3 _____
4 _____	*giving people a safe variety of a disease to protect them from the dangerous variety*

C

Are these sentences true or false?

1 Smallpox was a dangerous disease.
2 Mary Montagu lived for a time in Greece.
3 Mary Montagu brought blood to London.
4 Jenner was a farmer.
5 Jenner invented cowpox.
6 No one has caught smallpox since 1980.

Can we save the world?

1 All over the world we are losing biodiversity; different kinds of animal, bird, plant and insect life. There are many reasons for this: air and water pollution, growing numbers of people, hunting, global warming, disappearing habitats. What can we do? Can we save endangered species?

2 People have suggested different ways to save biodiversity. We can establish nature reserves or national parks, like the Wolong Mountain Reserve, the last home of the giant panda. We can recycle rubbish and reduce damage to our environment. New technology may help us to reduce pollution. We can control hunting and the sale of animal skins and bodies.

3 In the future, one way to save endangered species (and perhaps to bring back extinct animals) may be to clone them. Cloning is a special way of copying the genes of living or dead animals to grow a new animal. This has already happened. In 1996 scientists cloned a sheep. You will also know about cloning if you have seen the film *Jurassic Park*. However, many people think cloning will cause a lot of problems. In *Jurassic Park* a scientist cloned dinosaurs but the dinosaurs escaped from their reserve and attacked people.

4 One thing is certain. The problem of endangered species is bad and it is getting worse. Scientists think we are losing twenty to thirty species of plants and animals every day. If we do nothing, we will lose the battle and endangered species in their natural habitat will become extinct. Do we really want to live in a world without our favourite animals?

A

Read the text and match these titles with the correct paragraph.

a What we can do to save biodiversity
b Why we are losing biodiveristy
c Why we need to act quickly
d A new way to save endangered species

B

Find the words or expressions in the text for:

1 different kinds of animal, plant, bird and insect species
2 an increase in air temperatures
3 copying the genes of living or dead animals
4 if all the animals of a species are dead, the animal is …

C

What do these words in the text refer to?

1 this (paragraph 1, line 3)
2 them (paragraph 3, line 3)
3 this (paragraph 3 line 5)
4 their (paragraph 4, line 5)

A

Read the story of James Bartley. Choose the best title.

1 The *Star of the East*
2 The Stomach of a Whale
3 A Miraculous Escape

On the 25th August 1891, the *Star of the East* was sailing off the coast of Argentina. One of the sailors, Richard Bartley, was working on the ship when suddenly a big wave hit him. Bartley fell overboard and landed on something soft. Miraculously, he landed in the mouth of a twenty-metre long whale, which had been alongside the ship. Bartley went down and down inside the whale and arrived in its stomach. Then it got hot and hotter in the whale. Bartley couldn't move his legs or arms and he couldn't breathe. Finally, he became unconscious.

The crew of the *Star of the East* later caught the whale, but they did not know the lost sailor was inside. After the sailors had pulled the whale on board the ship, they started to cut it up. Suddenly they saw a movement inside the stomach. When they opened it, they found Bartley lying inside, unconscious. He had spent over twelve hours in the stomach of the whale. For two weeks Bartley was very ill but in the end he recovered completely. However, while he was lying in the beast's stomach, the acids in it had changed the colour of his skin and Bartley remained completely white for the rest of his life.

B

Read the story again and put these events in order.

Example: c = 1

a ... the sailors caught the whale
b ... Richard recovered completely but his skin was white
c ... the ship was sailing off the coast of Argentina
d ... he landed in the mouth of a whale
e ... the sailors opened the whale they found Bartley unconscious
f ... a wave hit Richard Bartley and he fell overboard

C

Fill in the gaps in exercise B with the words and expressions below.

Example: **a** = later

> when suddenly in the end miraculously
> later on the 25th of August

A

Read the text. Choose the best title.

1 The advantages of meat **2** Different kinds of meat **3** The disadvantages of meat

1   Most people like a steak or a hamburger. People now are eating more meat such as chicken, beef and lamb than in the past. For every one kilogram of meat we ate in 1950, we now eat two kilograms. To get this meat we keep many more meat animals such as cows, sheep, and rabbits than before. So meat is a good thing, isn't it? Read and learn.

2   … Yes and no. Meat is good protein but you mustn't eat too much. Meat can make us overweight. If we ate less meat and did more exercise, we wouldn't be so fat.

3   … Yes. Meat animals produce waste which pollutes water and land. A large farm of cows can produce more waste than a whole city. If we kept fewer meat animals, we would have a cleaner world and a better environment.

4   … Yes. Many countries don't have enough water now. When we produce 1 kg of beef, we need 7 kg of wheat, corn or other grain to feed the cows. And we need 7000 kg of water to grow the grain to feed the cows. If you didn't eat a hamburger for lunch, you would save enough water for 40 showers. That's a lot of water!

5   … You didn't? Let me explain. We are cutting down rain forests and destroying animal habitat to get farm land. We need even more land for meat than we need to grow other food. So demand for meat means less land for wild animals. If there were fewer cows and other meat animals, there would be more room for hunting animals such as tigers, leopards and cheetahs.

C

Put these sentences in the correct paragraph. Write the number.

a *Meat doesn't increase pollution, does it?* (Paragraph …)

b *Meat is a good food, isn't it?* (Paragraph …)

c *You knew that cows kill tigers, didn't you?* (Paragraph …)

d *Meat isn't bad for water, is it?* (Paragraph …)

B

Copy and complete this table

KIND	EXAMPLE 1	EXAMPLE 2
meat	*beef*	[1] _____
meat animal	[2] _____	*cows*
[3] _____	*wheat*	*corn*
[4] _____	*tiger*	*cheetah*

D

Choose the best sentence to complete the text:

We would probably be healthier and the world would be a better place if we …

1 stopped eating meat.
2 made the environment cleaner.
3 didn't keep cows.

A

Read the text. Find the paragraphs with information about:

1 communications satellites
2 the Pathfinder space probe
3 the advantages of unmanned space probes
4 plans for humans to go to Mars
5 the Earth's population
6 rocks from Mars
7 photographing Mars
8 why Mars is the best place to live

Exploring Mars

A

In 1999, the population of the earth reached six billion (6,000,000,000). It will probably reach eight billion in another fifty years. In the future, we may have to find new places for people to live because there might not be enough room on Earth. People may go to live in space colonies or they might go to live on the other planets. Scientists think that Mars will be the best place to live because it is the closest planet to the earth and it will be easier to travel there. The temperature, gravity and environment are not too different from Earth. Another advantage is that there is probably water there.

B

Before people can live on Mars, we need more information about it. The North American Space Agency, NASA, is planning to send more space probes to explore Mars. Space probes are better than manned space craft because space travel over long distances is difficult and dangerous for humans and takes a long time. There are, of course, no people on board space probes and scientists on Earth send signals to the probes to control them. This takes a long time. When the Pathfinder space probe landed on Mars in 1997, it took 11 minutes for signals to travel to and from Earth. Another difficulty is that the space probes do not have a lot of energy to send their information back to Earth.

C

It is important to improve communications between Mars and Earth. NASA scientists want to have communications satellites around Mars. When they are in position, they will help scientists to send and receive signals from the exploration probes more easily. Cameras on the satellites will photograph Mars and scientists will make better maps. Communications satellites will also help NASA with its plan for a space probe to bring rock back from Mars.

D

When more information is known about Mars, humans might be able to explore the planet themselves. NASA scientist Chad Edwards said: "If we have to carry everything with us, we'll never get there." NASA's plan is to send unmanned space probes first that will produce energy, water, fuel and air on Mars. Humans will then use these supplies during their stay there.

B

Write questions for these answers, using Why, When, How long, What and Who.

1 ...... ? – In another fifty years.
2 ...... ? – There might not be enough room on Earth.
3 ...... ? – NASA is planning to send more space probes to explore Mars.
4 ...... ? – Eleven minutes.
5 ...... ? – Energy, water, fuel and air.

C

Answer these questions.

1 Find two reasons why unmanned space probes are better than manned space craft.
2 Find two reasons why it is difficult to use unmanned space probes.
3 Find three reasons why NASA scientists want communications satellites around Mars.

Mini-dictionary

This mini-dictionary will help you to understand all the words that are either important to remember or necessary to do the activities. Remember that you don't have to understand every word when you read a text. We recommend that you refer to the **Longman Active Study Dictionary** for words not included here. Remember that this mini-dictionary is not a substitute for a complete dictionary.

Abbreviations used in this mini-dictionary:

adj = adjective
adv = adverb
conj = conjunction

n = noun
no pl = no plural form
pl = plural

prep = preposition
pron = pronoun
v = verb

Aa

ability /əˈbɪləti/ *n* the power or knowledge to do something: *Doctors now have the ability to keep people alive much longer.*

acid rain /ˌæsɪd ˈreɪn/ *n* (no pl) rain which causes damage to trees and plants because it contains acid put into the air by factories

advantage /ədˈvɑːntɪdʒ/ *n* something that helps a person: *It is an advantage to speak several languages.*

adventure /ədˈventʃə/ *n* an exciting experience when dangerous or unusual things happen

advertising /ˈædvətaɪzɪŋ/ *n* notices in public places or short films to give people information about something

afraid /əˈfreɪd/ *adj* feeling fear: *Are you afraid of the dark?*

air pollution /ˈeə pəˌluːʃən/ *n* (no pl) the process of making the air dirty or dangerous

airport /ˈeəpɔːt/ *n* a place that you arrive at or leave from when travelling by plane

amazing /əˈmeɪzɪŋ/ *adj* surprising and exciting: *What amazing news!*

ancient /ˈeɪnʃənt/ *adj* very old: *an ancient building*

anger /ˈæŋgə/ *n* (no pl) the feeling of being very annoyed

angry /ˈæŋgri/ *adj* feeling very annoyed: *I'm very angry with them. adv* **angrily**

argue /ˈɑːgjuː/ *v* to disagree: *They often argued about money.*

army /ˈɑːmi/ *n* (pl **armies**) a large number of soldiers fighting together

art gallery /ˈɑːt ˌgæləri/ *n* a room or building where you can look at paintings and other types of art

astronaut /ˈæstrənɔːt/ *n* someone who travels in space

athletics /æθˈletɪks/ *n* (no pl) sports in which people run, jump or throw things to see who is best

atmosphere /ˈætməsfɪə/ *n* (no pl) **1** the air surrounding the Earth **2** a feeling that a place or a group of people give you: *a relaxed atmosphere*

attack /əˈtæk/ *n, v* fight against someone or harm them: *He was attacked in the street.*

autumn /ˈɔːtəm/ *n* the season when leaves fall off the trees

avoid /əˈvɔɪd/ *v* to keep away from a person, place or thing: *Are you trying to avoid me?*

Bb

backpack /ˈbækpæk/ *n* a bag that you carry on your back

bad /bæd/ *adj* (**worse, worst**) **1** not good or pleasant: *We had some bad news yesterday - our dog died.* **2** food that is bad is not safe to eat because it is not fresh: *The milk has gone bad. adv* **badly**

ball /bɔːl/ *n* a round object that you throw, kick or hit in a game: *a tennis ball*

bandage /ˈbændɪdʒ/ *n* a long piece of cloth that is tied on to your body to cover a wound

basketball /ˈbɑːskɪtbɔːl/ *n* a game in which two teams try to win points by throwing a ball through a net

bat /bæt/ *n* **1** a piece of wood used to hit the ball in games such as baseball, cricket and table tennis **2** a small animal with wings that flies around at night

bathroom /ˈbɑːθruːm/ *n* a room where there is a bath, shower and usually a toilet

beach /biːtʃ/ *n* (pl **beaches**) an area of sand or stones at the edge of the sea

bear /beə/ *n* a large and sometimes fierce wild animal with a thick coat

beat /biːt/ *v* (**beat, beaten, beating**) **1** to defeat or have a better result than

someone **2** to hit someone or something many times **3** to move regularly many times: *Her heart was beating fast.*

beautiful /ˈbjuːtɪfəl/ *adj* **1** very attractive: *a beautiful woman* **2** very nice: *What a beautiful day! adv* **beautifully**

beauty /ˈbjuːti/ *n* the quality of being beautiful: *the beauty of the Swiss mountains*

become /bɪˈkʌm/ *v* (**became, become becoming**) to begin to be something

bedroom /ˈbedruːm/ *n* a room for sleeping in

behaviour /bɪˈheɪvjə/ *n* (no pl) the way a person acts: *What bad behaviour!*

believe /bɪˈliːv/ *v* **1** to think that something is true **2** to think that someone is telling the truth **3** to have an opinion: *I believe we will win the game.*

bend /bend/ *v* (**bent, bent, bending**) **1** to move the top part of your body down towards the ground **2** to move something into a curved position

bicycle /ˈbaɪsɪkəl/ *n* a vehicle with two wheels that you ride by pushing pedals with your feet

bird sanctuary /ˈbɜːd ˌsæŋktʃuəri, -tʃəri/ *n* a protected area for birds

bite /baɪt/ *v* (**bit, bitten, biting**) to cut or wound something with the teeth

blood /blʌd/ *n* (no pl) the red liquid in your body

boar /bɔː/ *n* a wild pig

boat /bəʊt/ *n* a small open ship: *a fishing boat*

boots /buːts/ *n* a shoe that covers your foot and ankle

boring /ˈbɔːrɪŋ/ *adj* not interesting: *This book's so boring - I don't think I'll ever finish it.*

brave /breɪv/ *adj* not afraid or showing fear: *a brave soldier. adv* **bravely**

bravery /ˈbreɪvəri/ *n* (no pl) willingness to do dangerous things without feeling afraid

Mini-dictionary

breathe /briːð/ *v* to take air into your body and let it out again through your nose or mouth

breed /briːd/ *v* (**bred, bred, breeding**) (used about animals) to produce young

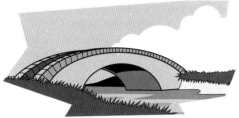

bridge /brɪdʒ/ *n* a road or railway line built over something: *a bridge across the river*

bright /braɪt/ *adj* **1** sending out strong, shining light **2** having a strong, clear colour **3** quick at learning things

brilliant /ˈbrɪljənt/ *adj* **1** brilliant light or colour is very bright and strong **2** very good, intelligent or skilful: *He's a brilliant footballer.* *adv* **brilliantly**

brochure /ˈbrəʊʃə, -ʃʊə/ *n* a thin book giving information or advertising something

build /bɪld/ *v* (**built, built, building**) to make something by putting pieces together: *The house is built of stone.*

burn /bɜːn/ *v* (**burned** or **burnt, burned** or **burnt, burning**) **1** to be on fire: *The house is burning.* **2** to hurt yourself or part of your body with something very hot

burn /bɜːn/ *n* a wound or mark on your body caused by fire or by touching something very hot

bus /bʌs/ *n* a large vehicle that people pay to travel on

Cc

cable /ˈkeɪbəl/ *n* wires that carry electricity or telephone calls

calmly /ˈkɑːmli/ *adv* in a quiet and peaceful way: *He sat down calmly.*

can /kæn/ or **tin** /tɪn/ *n* a container made of metal. Food in cans is called canned food

canoeing /kəˈnuːɪŋ/ *n* a sport in which people travel or race in a narrow, light boat

capture /ˈkæptʃə/ *v* to take someone as a prisoner: *They captured four enemy soldiers.*

car /kɑː/ *n* a vehicle with four wheels and an engine designed to be used by a small number of people

carbon dioxide /ˌkɑːbən daɪˈɒksaɪd/ *n* a gas produced when people or animals breathe out or when carbon is burned in air

career /kəˈrɪə/ *n* a person's working life: *Our teacher gave us some advice about different careers.*

catch /kætʃ/ *v* (**caught, caught, catching**) **1** to get in the hand and hold: *She threw the ball and I caught it.* **2** to run after and take hold of: *We ran after the dog and caught it.* **3** to get: *I caught a cold. She caught the train here.*

cathedral /kəˈθiːdrəl/ *n* a very large church which is usually the main church in the area

cave /keɪv/ *n* a hollow place under the ground or in rocks or the side of a mountain

centipede /ˈsentɪpiːd/ *n* a creature like a worm with a lot of very small legs

century /ˈsentʃəri/ *n* (pl **centuries**) (a period of) one hundred years: *It was built in the 19th century.*

cereal /ˈsɪəriəl/ *n* **1** (no pl) breakfast food that is made from grain and usually eaten with milk **2** (pl) a plant grown to produce grain for food, for example wheat or rice: *Their farm grows mainly cereals.*

champion /ˈtʃæmpiən/ *n* someone who is the best at something, especially a game or a sport

championship /ˈtʃæmpiənʃɪp/ *n* a competition to find out who is the best at something

cheap /tʃiːp/ *adj* costing only a little money: *A bicycle is much cheaper than a car.*

chemical /ˈkemɪkəl/ *n* a substance, especially one used in or made by chemistry

child /tʃaɪld/ *n* (pl **children**) **1** a young person **2** a son or a daughter: *Both our children are married now.*

childhood /ˈtʃaɪldhʊd/ *n* the time when you are a child

chimney /ˈtʃɪmni/ *n* a pipe that allows smoke to go up and out of a building

chimney sweep /ˈtʃɪmni swiːp/ *n* a person who cleans chimneys

cinema /ˈsɪnəmə/ *n* a building where you go to see films

claw /klɔː/ *n* one of the sharp, hard points on the foot of a bird or animal

clean /kliːn/ *adj* **1** not dirty: *Have you got a clean shirt?* **2** not yet used: *A clean piece of paper.*

clearly /ˈklɪəli/ *adv* **1** in a clear way: *Please speak more clearly.* **2** without any doubt: *He is clearly very clever.*

clever /ˈklevə/ *adj* quick at learning and understanding things

climbing /ˈklaɪmɪŋ/ *n* a sport in which people climb hills or mountains

clothes /kləʊðz, kləʊz/ *pl n* things we wear such as shirts or trousers

cloudy /ˈklaʊdi/ *adj* (**cloudier, cloudiest**) having lot of clouds: *a cloudy day*

club /klʌb/ *n* **1** a group of people who meet together for some purpose: *A football club* **2** a large heavy stick

coffee /ˈkɒfi/ *n* **1** (no pl) a hot brown drink made from coffee beans **2** (pl) a cup of coffee: *Two coffees please.*

colony /ˈkɒləni/ *n* (pl **colonies**) **1** a country that is under the control of another country **2** a group of people who live in a colony

colourful /ˈkʌləfəl/ *adj* bright, having lots of colours: *colourful clothes*

come back /kʌm ˈbæk/ (**came, come, coming**) *v* to return: *Her parents told her to come back home before ten o'clock.*

come up to /kʌm ˈʌp tə/ (**came, come, coming**) *v* **1** to come near to someone or something **2** to equal: *His performance didn't come up to his usual standard.*

common /ˈkɒmən/ *adj* **1** exists in large numbers or happens often: *Red cars are common this year.* **2** shared by two or more people: *We have a common interest in sailing.*

communications /kəˌmjuːnɪˈkeɪʃənz/ *pl n* road, rail, telephone, radio and all other ways of sending information between places

completely /kəmˈpliːtli/ *adv* in every way, totally

computer /kəmˈpjuːtə/ *n* a machine that stores and organises large amounts of information

concert /ˈkɒnsət/ *n* a piece of music played in public for a lot of people: *I went to a great pop concert last night.*

corn /kɔːn/ *n* (no pl) the seed of grain plants, including wheat and maize

cosmonaut /ˈkɒzmənɔːt/ *n* a Russian astronaut (someone who travels in space)

cotton /ˈkɒtn/ *n* (no pl) a plant grown in hot countries for the fine white cotton threads and which are made into thread or material: *She sewed the cotton dress with cotton.*

country /ˈkʌntri/ *n* **1** (pl **countries**) an area ruled by one government: *France and Germany are European countries.* **2** (no pl) the land that is not in a town: *He lives in the country.*

court /kɔːt/ *n* an open space where games are played: *a tennis court*

crash /kræʃ/ *v* **1** to move noisily **2** to make a sudden loud noise **3** (of a car or plane) to have an accident: *The car crashed into the tree.*

creative /kriˈeɪtɪv/ *adj* a creative person is good at thinking of new ideas or ways of doing things *adv* **creatively**

creativity /kriːeɪˈtɪvəti/ *n* ability to produce and use new ideas

crime /kraɪm/ *n* something that is wrong and can be punished by the law: *Stealing is a crime.*

crowded /ˈkraʊdɪd/ *adj* full of people: *I don't like the market; it is too crowded.*

curious /ˈkjʊərɪəs/ *adj* **1** wanting to know about people and things: *It is good to be curious about the world around you.* **2** strange or odd: *a curious fact*

cycling /ˈsaɪklɪŋ/ *n* the sport of riding a bicycle: *John goes cycling at weekends.*

cyclist /ˈsaɪklɪst/ *n* a person who rides a bike

Dd

damage /ˈdæmɪdʒ/ *n* (no pl) harm, especially to things

damage /ˈdæmɪdʒ/ *v* to hurt; cause damage to: *The car was badly damaged in the accident.*

dangerous /ˈdeɪndʒərəs/ *adj* likely to harm people: *a dangerous driver*

dark /dɑːk/ *adj* **1** like night; not bright and light: *It was getting dark.* **2** of a deep colour, nearer to black than white: *He wore a dark suit.* **3** the lack of light: *We can't see in the dark.*

dead /ded/ *adj* not living: *My grandfather has been dead for ten years.*

deadly /ˈdedli/ *adj* (**deadlier, deadliest**) causing death: *This seed is deadly if you eat it.*

death /deθ/ *n* the state of being dead or the act of dying: *the death of his father*

debut /ˈdeɪbjuː/ *n* the first time that a performer or sports player performs in public: *He made his debut for the school team last week.*

decide /dɪˈsaɪd/ *v* to make a choice or judgement about something. **decide to do something**: *She decided to sell the house.*

delicate /ˈdelɪkət/ *adj* easily damaged or broken

delicious /dɪˈlɪʃəs/ *adj* good to eat: *This soup is delicious.*

democracy /dɪˈmɒkrəsi/ *n* the system in which everyone in a country can vote to choose the government *adj* **democratic**

desperate /ˈdespərət/ *adj* ready to do anything to get what you want: *The man lost in the desert was desperate for water.* *adv* **desperately**

destroy /dɪˈstrɔɪ/ *v* to break up or get rid of completely: *The fire destroyed all my books.*

destruction /dɪˈstrʌkʃən/ *n* (no pl) when something is destroyed

develop /dɪˈveləp/ *v* **1** to grow: *The fighting could develop into a war. An insect which develops wings* **2** to make something grow or improve: *plans to develop industry in the area*

development /dɪˈveləpmənt/ *n* **1** the latest in a number of real or imaginary events **2** (no pl) growth: *a child's development, the development of industry*

die /daɪ/ *v* to stop living: *She died last year.*

dinner /ˈdɪnə/ *n* the main meal of the day, usually eaten in the evening

dirty /ˈdɜːti/ *adj* not clean: *The children got dirty playing outside.*

disadvantage /ˌdɪsədˈvɑːntɪdʒ/ *n* something that makes things more difficult for you: *The disadvantages of not having a car*

disappear /ˌdɪsəˈpɪə/ *v* to go away or go out of sight suddenly: *The boy disappeared round the corner.*

disco /ˈdɪskəʊ/ *n* a place or event where people dance to popular music

disease /dɪˈziːz/ *n* an illness, especially a serious one

doctor /ˈdɒktə/ *n* someone whose job is to treat people who are ill

dolphin /ˈdɒlfɪn/ *n* a large sea animal that swims around in groups

dream /driːm/ *v* (**dreamt** or **dreamed, dreamt** or **dreamed, dreaming**) **1** to imagine things when you are asleep: *I dreamed about my teacher last night.* **2** to imagine something nice: *I dream of being the best footballer in town.*

dream /driːm/ *n* **1** something that you imagine when you are asleep: *a frightening dream* **2** something nice that you imagine or that you want to do: *It's my dream to come first in the race.*

drive /draɪv/ *v* (**drove, driven, driving**) to control a motor vehicle and make it move: *Jane drives a blue car.*

dynamic /daɪˈnæmɪk/ *adj* full of new and exciting ideas and very active: *Our teacher is very dynamic: she wants to change everything.*

Ee

eagle /ˈiːgəl/ *n* a large bird that lives in mountains and kills small birds for food

east /iːst/ *adj, adv* the direction from which the sun comes up in the morning: *Our house faces east. There is a strong east wind* (= from the east).

ecology /ɪˈkɒlədʒi/ *n* (no pl) the study of the way plants, animals and people relate to each other and their surroundings

emotion /ɪˈməʊʃən/ *n* a strong feeling such as love or hate

emotional /ɪˈməʊʃənəl/ *adj* **1** showing your feelings to other people **2** making people have strong feelings **3** connected with your feelings *adv* **emotionally**

endangered /ɪnˈdeɪndʒəd/ *adj* (usually about plant or animal species) something that might not exist soon: *The whale is an endangered species.*

energetic /enəˈdʒetɪk/ *adj* very active and able to work hard *adv* **energetically**

energy /ˈenədʒi/ *n* (no pl) power to do things or make things work: *I have no energy left after playing football. Coal and gas give us energy for heating, lighting or moving things.*

enormous /ɪˈnɔːməs/ *adj* very big: *an enormous plate of food*

enthusiasm /ɪnˈθjuːziæzəm/ *n* (no pl) a strong feeling of interest, excitement or admiration about something

enthusiastic /ɪnˌθjuːzɪˈæstɪk/ *adj* very keen on something or interested in it *adv* **enthusiastically**

environment /ɪnˈvaɪərənmənt/ *n* (no pl) **1** the conditions of the earth and of the people surrounding you: *Children need a happy home environment.* **2** the world of land, sea and air that you live in: *Cutting down too many trees is bad for the environment.*

establish /ɪˈstæblɪʃ/ *v* **1** to start a company, organisation, system or situation that is intended to exist or continue for a long time: *My grandfather established the family business in 1938.* **2** to find out the facts that will prove if something is true: *The detective established that James was not there at the time of the murder.*

exchange /ɪksˈtʃeɪndʒ/ *v* to give something to someone in return for something else: *This skirt is too small. Maybe the shop will exchange it.*

exciting /ɪkˈsaɪtɪŋ/ *adj* able to make someone happy or interested, not boring: *My skiing holiday was really exciting.*

exercise /ˈeksəsaɪz/ *n* **1** using your body to make it stronger or more healthy: *Running is good exercise.* **2** a piece of work given in school: *I've just finished a difficult maths exercise.*

exhaust /ɪgˈzɔːst/ *n* (no pl.) the burnt gases that come out of an engine

Mini-dictionary

exist /ɪɡˈzɪst/ v to be: *The house where I was born no longer exists.*

extinct /ɪkˈstɪŋkt/ adj (of a plant or animal) no longer exists: *The elephant is becoming extinct.*

Ff

factory /ˈfæktəri/ n (pl **factories**) a place where things are made, often by machines

fall /fɔːl/ v (**fell, fallen, falling**) to drop to a lower place: *My book fell onto the floor.*

fantastic /fænˈtæstɪk/ adj **1** extremely good, attractive or enjoyable **2** strange or unreal: *fantastic stories of ghosts and monsters*

farm /fɑːm/ n land on which people grow food or keep animals

farmer /ˈfɑːmə/ n someone who owns or manages a farm

fascinating /ˈfæsɪneɪtɪŋ/ adj extremely interesting: *History is a fascinating subject.*

fast /fɑːst/ adj moving or happening very fast: *The new train to London is very fast. adv* **fast**: *You're learning fast.*

field /fiːld/ n a piece of ground, usually with a fence or wall around it, used for growing crops or keeps animals: *a field of wheat*

figure /ˈfɪɡə/ n **1** a number such as 3 or 4 **2** a shape, usually the shape of the human body: *I can see a tall figure by the door.*

find out /ˌfaɪnd ˈaʊt/ v (**found, found, finding**) to discover

flamingo /fləˈmɪŋɡəʊ/ n a tropical bird with long legs, pink feathers and a long neck

food /fuːd/ n (no pl) things that people and animals eat.

football /ˈfʊtbɔːl/ n **1** a game in which two teams try to kick a ball into a net **2** the ball used in this game n **footballer** a person whose job is to play football

foreign /ˈfɒrən/ adj of or from a country that is not your country: *a foreign language*

forest /ˈfɒrɪst/ n an area where a lot of trees grow together

free /friː/ adj **1** able to do what you like: *You are free to leave at any time.* **2** not costing any money: *I got a free ticket to the match* **3** not in prison

freedom /ˈfriːdəm/ n being able to do what you want without being a prisoner and without being under another person's control

fridge /frɪdʒ/ n a machine like an electric cupboard that you keep in your kitchen and use for keeping food cool and fresh

frightened /ˈfraɪtnd/ adj afraid: *He's frightened of dogs.*

fruit /fruːt/ pl n something such as an apple, banana or strawberry which grows on a plant or tree and contains seeds

fur /fɜː/ n the soft hair on some animals, such as cats and rabbits: *a fur coat (a coat made of fur)*

furniture /ˈfɜːnɪtʃə/ n (no pl) objects such as chairs, tables, and wardrobes that you use in a room or office

Gg

galaxy /ˈɡæləksi/ n one of the large groups of stars which form the universe *adj* **galactic**

generator /ˈdʒenəreɪtə/ n a machine that usually produces electricity

get /ɡet/ v (**got, got, getting**) **1** to take, have or buy: *I got a letter from Maria this morning. I must get some fruit in the market.* **2** to become: *I got angry with him.* **3** to make be or happen: *He got the shirt clean in hot water.* **4** to arrive: *When he got to the station, the train had arrived.* **5** must: *I've got to see him today.*

get around /ˌɡet əˈraʊnd/ v to move or travel from place to place: *He doesn't get around since his accident.*

get down /ˌɡet ˈdaʊn/ v to climb off something

get married /ˌɡet ˈmærid/ v to marry someone

get on /ˌɡet ˈɒn/ v to climb on to something like a train or a bus

get out /ˌɡet ˈaʊt/ v to leave or escape from: *The prisoner got out of the prison.*

get up /ˌɡet ˈʌp/ v to get out of bed

ghost /ɡəʊst/ n the form of a dead person which a living person thinks he/she can see

giant /ˈdʒaɪənt/ adj very large or big: *a giant snake*

giant /ˈdʒaɪənt/ n a very large person, usually only one talked about in stories

glass /ɡlɑːs/ n **1** (no pl) a clear hard substance used for making windows or bottles. **2** (pl) a container made of glass used for drinking.

global warming /ˌɡləʊbəl ˈwɔːmɪŋ/ n (no pl) a general increase in temperatures caused by increased amounts of carbon dioxide in the atmosphere

good /ɡʊd/ adj (**better, best**) **1** of a high standard or quality: *a good school* **2** skilful or successful at something: *She's good at tennis.* **3** well-behaved: *They're very good children.*

go on /ˌɡəʊ ˈɒn/ v to happen: *What's going on here?*

go on to do /ˌɡəʊ ˌɒn tʊ ˈduː/ v to do a second action after finishing the first: *He won the first match and went on to win the final.*

go out /ˌɡəʊ ˈaʊt/ v to leave

go up /ˌɡəʊ ˈʌp/ v to increase in number: *Prices went up a lot last year.*

golf /ɡɒlf/ n (no pl) a game in which you try to hit a small hard ball into a hole in the ground using a club or type of stick

gorilla /ɡəˈrɪlə/ n a very large, strong animal which looks like an enormous monkey

grass /ɡrɑːs/ n (no pl) a common plant with thin leaves which covers fields and gardens: *We sat on the grass to have our picnic.*

gravity /ˈɡrævəti/ n (no pl) the force which holds you to Earth: *When you let go of something, gravity makes it fall to earth.*

grow /ɡrəʊ/ (**grow, grew, grown**) **1** to get bigger: *Children grow quickly. I am growing an orange tree. (=I have planted the seed and I am waiting for it to get bigger)* **2** to become: *The weather grew colder.*

grow up /ˌɡrəʊ ˈʌp/ v to become adult: *I want to be a doctor when I grow up. I grew up (=became an adult) in Paris.*

Hh

habitat /ˈhæbɪtæt/ n the place where a plant or animal naturally lives: *Many animals have been forced to leave their natural habitat.*

happy /ˈhæpi/ adj feeling pleased and cheerful because something good has happened *adv* **happily**

hard /hɑːd/ adj **1** not moving or soft when touched; firm, like rock or metal: *The ground is too hard to dig.* **2** difficult to do or understand: *a hard exam*

hard /hɑːd/ adv using a lot of effort or force: *She worked very hard to pass her exams.*

haunted house /ˌhɔːntɪd ˈhaʊs/ n a house believed to be visited by ghosts

have to /ˈhæv tʊ, tə/ v (**had, had, having**) must: *We have to leave now, so we can catch the bus.*

head /hed/ n **1** the top part of your body where your brain and face are **2** your mind **3** the leader of a group or organisation: *the head of the environmental action group*

health /helθ/ *n* (no pl) the state of your body; how you are: *His health is not very good.* (he is often ill)

healthy /'helθi/ *adj* (**healthier, healthiest**) having good health: *You look very healthy. It is healthy* (good for your body) *to eat fruit.*

height /haɪt/ *n* how tall or far from the ground something is: *He measured the height of the bridge.*

helmet /'helmɪt/ *n* a hard hat you wear to stop your head being hurt

hippopotamus /hɪpə'pɒtəməs/ *n* a large, grey African animal with a big head and fat body which lives near water (informal **hippo**)

hockey /'hɒki/ *n* **1** BrE a game played on grass in which two teams try to hit a ball into a goal using sticks **2** AmE a game played on ice in which two teams try to hit a hard flat object (puck) into a goal

hold /həʊld/ *v* (**held, held, holding**) **1** to have something in your hands or arms: *The little girl held the toy tightly in her arms.* **2** to keep something in a particular position: *Can you hold this picture up for a minute, please?* **3** to have something inside: *This bottle holds two litres.* **4** to have a record in something: *She holds the world record for high jump.*

homeless /'həʊmlɪs/ *adj* having nowhere to live

horn /hɔːn/ *n* **1** one of two hard pieces sticking out of the heads of some animals **2** an instrument on a car or bus that gives a short, loud sound as a warning: *The taxi blew its horn.*

horror /'hɒrə/ *n* great fear and shock: *The man saw with horror that there had been a bad accident.*

horse /hɔːs/ *n* a large animal with four legs that people ride on

horse-riding /'hɔːs raɪdɪŋ/ *n* the sport of riding horses for pleasure

huge /hjuːdʒ/ *adj* enormous; very large: *We ate a huge meal.*

hummingbird /'hʌmɪŋbɜːd/ *n* a small, brightly coloured bird which moves its wings so quickly it makes a musical noise

hunt /hʌnt/ *v* to chase and kill animals for food or sport

Ii

impressive /ɪm'presɪv/ *adj* causing strong feelings or thought: *Her work is very impressive.*

improve /ɪm'pruːv/ *v* to become or to make something better: *I want to improve my English.*

incredible /ɪn'kredɪbəl/ *adj* **1** extremely good, large or impressive: *The show was incredible!* **2** too strange to be believed: *She told me an incredible story about a werewolf.*

industry /'ɪndəstri/ *n* (pl **industries**) making things in factories: *Our town has a lot of industry.*

intention /ɪn'tenʃən/ *n* something that you plan to do: *John's intention is to study medicine at university.*

invent /ɪn'vent/ *v* to think of and plan something new which did not exist before

Jj

join /dʒɔɪn/ *v* **1** become a member of a group or organisation. **2** to connect things together: *Join the two pieces of wood with strong glue.* **3** where roads, rivers or parts of something come together

judo /'dʒuːdəʊ/ *n* (no pl) a sport from Japan in which you try to throw your opponent to the ground

Kk

karate /kə'rɑːti/ *n* (no pl) a sport from Japan in which you fight using your hands and feet

keep out /ˌkiːp 'aʊt/ *v* (**kept, kept, keeping**) to stop someone from going inside a place

kingdom /'kɪŋdəm/ *n* a country ruled by a king

kitchen /'kɪtʃɪn/ *n* the room in a house or restaurant where food is prepared to eat

knee /niː/ *n* the joint in the middle of the leg where the leg bends

knight /naɪt/ *n* a noble soldier of the middle ages trained to fight on a horse

Ll

lake /leɪk/ *n* a big pool of water with land around it

land /lænd/ *v* **1** to come to the ground or the land from the air or water: *The plane will land in five minutes.* **2** to bring the plane or ship to the ground from the air or water: *He landed the plane at the airport.* **landing** *n*: *The plane made a safe landing.*

large /lɑːdʒ/ *adj* very big

layer /'leɪə/ *n* a covering that is spread on top of another thing or in between two other things: *This cake has a layer of chocolate in the middle.*

length /leŋθ/ *n* (no pl) the distance from one end of a thing to another; how long something is: *Mary's dress is not the right length; it is too short.*

levitate /'levɪteɪt/ *v* to rise and float in the air (by magic)

lift /lɪft/ *v* to pick something up: *Can you lift the other end of the table, please?*

light /laɪt/ *n* (no pl) **1** the force from the sun that allows our eyes to see: *There's more light near the window.* **2** a thing that gives out light: *Turn off the lights when you go to bed.*

light /laɪt/ *adj* **1** not dark in colour; pale: *a light blue sky* **2** easy to lift; not heavy: *The basket is very light. I can pick it up easily.* **3** not great in amount: *The traffic is very light this evening.*

lightbulb /'laɪtbʌlb/ *n* a round glass object with a wire inside that gives out light: *She put a new lightbulb in the lamp.*

litter /'lɪtə/ *n* (no pl) waste paper and other things lying on the ground: *There was litter everywhere on the streets of the town.*

lizard /'lɪzəd/ *n* an animal that has four short legs and a skin like a snake

logic /'lɒdʒɪk/ *n* a set of sensible and correct reasons: *There is no logic in your argument.*

logical /'lɒdʒɪkəl/ *adj* reasonable and sensible: *He is the logical choice for captain of the team.* *adv* **logically**

lonely /'ləʊnli/ *adj* (**lonelier, loneliest**) unhappy because you are alone: *He was lonely without his wife.*

long /lɒŋ/ *adj* **1** measures a great length from one end to the other: *She's got long hair.* **2** continuing for a great amount of time: *It was a long, boring film.*

look back /ˌlʊk 'bæk/ *v* to think about something that happened in the past: *When I look back at that time, I was very unhappy.*

look for /'lʊk fə, fɔː/ *v* to try to find something or someone: *I'm looking for my key.*

look up (words) /ˌlʊk 'ʌp/ *v* to find a piece of information in a book, such as a dictionary

loris /'lɔːrɪs/ *n* a South American mammal which lives in trees

lose /luːz/ *v* (**lost, lost, losing**) **1** not to have something anymore and not to know where it is: *I can't find my watch. I must have lost it.* **2** not to do well; not to win: *Our team lost the football match.*

lynx /lɪŋks/ *n* a large wild cat with no tail that lives in forests

Mm

mad /mæd/ *adj* (**madder, maddest**) **1** ill in the mind **2** very foolish: *You're mad to drive that fast.* **3** very angry: *She was mad at him for being late.*

Mini-dictionary

magnificent /mæg'nɪfɪsənt/ *adj* very great; very fine: *What a magnificent building!*

mammal /'mæməl/ *n* an animal that is fed on its mother's milk when it is young, for example a cow, lion or human baby

manufacture /ˌmænjʊ'fæktʃə/ *v* to make things in large numbers, usually by machines: *We manufacture cars in our factory.*

map /mæp/ *n* a drawing of an area which shows cities, rivers, roads etc.

marsh /mɑːʃ/ *n* (pl **marshes**) low, wet ground: *When they crossed the marsh their shoes sank into the soft ground.*

match /mætʃ/ *n* (pl **matches**) a game between two people or two teams: *a football match*

material /mə'tɪəriəl/ *adj* solid and physical; not spiritual: *Food is a material need.*

message /'mesɪdʒ/ *n* news or an order sent from one person to another: *I have sent mother a message to say I will be late home.*

metal /'metəl/ *n* a hard substance such as gold, steel or silver

migrate /maɪ'greɪt/ *v* **1** birds or animals which migrate fly to a warmer place for winter and return in spring **2** to go to live in another place usually to find work

Milky Way /ˌmɪlki 'weɪ/ *n* the pale, white band of stars that can be seen across the sky at night

mine /maɪn/ *n* a deep hole in the ground from which people take out coal, iron, gold etc.

mine /maɪn/ *v* to dig out something from a mine: *They were mining coal.*

miner /'maɪnə/ *n* a person who works in a mine

mineral /'mɪnərəl/ *n* a substance like iron, coal, or oil which is taken out of the ground

miraculously /mɪ'rækjʊləsli/ *adv* in a surprising and wonderful way

modern /'mɒdən/ *adj* new; in the style that is popular now

monster /'mɒnstə/ *n* a large, ugly, frightening creature

moon /muːn/ *n* a large round object that moves around a planet: *How many moons does Jupiter have?*

motorbike /'məʊtəbaɪk/ *n* a vehicle with two wheels and an engine.

mountain /'maʊntɪn/ *n* a very high hill: *We went to the Swiss mountains on holiday.*

move /muːv/ *v* **1** to change the position of something from one place to another **2** to go to live in another place: *They moved to London last year.*

murder /'mɜːdə/ *verb* to kill a person when you have decided to do it

murderer /'mɜːdərə/ *n* a person who murders someone

museum /mju'ziːəm/ *n* a building where you can go and see important things connected with science, history etc.

mysterious /mɪ'stɪəriəs/ *adj* strange and difficult to understand and explain *adv* **mysteriously**

mystery /'mɪstəri/ *n* **1** something that is difficult to explain or understand **2** a story, often about a murder, in which events are not explained until the end: *the Sherlock Holmes mysteries*

mystic /'mɪstɪk/ *n* a person who studies religion or who has spiritual knowledge

Nn

natural /'nætʃərəl/ *adj* **1** normal or usual: *It's natural for children to be noisy.* **2** not made or caused by humans

nature reserve /'neɪtʃə rɪˌzɜːv/ *n* an area of land in which plants and animals are protected

nearly /'nɪəli/ *adv* almost: *We have nearly finished.*

neighbour /'neɪbə/ *n* someone who lives near you: *a next door neighbour*

nervous /'nɜːvəs/ *adj* worried or afraid: *She was nervous about travelling alone.*

nest /nest/ *n* a home built by a bird or by some animals or insects: *The bird laid three eggs in her nest.*

net /net/ *n* material with open spaces between knotted thread, string or wire: *The footballer kicked the ball into the back of the net.*

never /'nevə/ *adv* not at any time or not once: *I've never been to Germany.*

newspaper /'njuːspeɪpə/ *n* a set of sheets of paper containing news and advertisements, which is sold every day or week: *an evening newspaper*

noise /nɔɪz/ *n* a loud sound, often unpleasant: *Planes make a lot of noise. My car's making strange noises.*

noisy /'nɔɪzi/ *adj* (**noisier, noisiest**): loud: *"What a noisy class you are!" said the teacher.*

noisily /'nɔɪzɪli/ *adv* in a loud way

notice /'nəʊtɪs/ *v* to see: *The prisoner noticed that the door was open and ran away.*

nuclear power /ˌnjuːkliə 'paʊə/ *n* power, usually electricity, which is obtained from nuclear energy

nurse /nɜːs/ *n* a person, often a woman, who is trained to help doctors and look after people when they are sick or old: *She works as a nurse in a hospital.*

nurse /nɜːs/ *v* to care for sick people: *She nursed her mother when she was ill.*

Oo

occasional /ə'keɪʒənəl/ *adj* happening sometimes but not often *adv* **occasionally**

often /'ɒfən, 'ɒftən/ *adv* many times: *I often go to bed early.*

old-fashioned /ˌəʊld 'fæʃənd/ *adj* not common any more: *old-fashioned clothes*

orbit /'ɔːbɪt/ *v* to move in an orbit around something: *The space craft orbited the moon.*

oxygen /'ɒksɪdʒən/ *n* a gas in the air that all living things breathe in order to survive.

ozone layer /'əʊzəʊn ˌleɪə/ *n* (no pl) a layer of gases which protects the earth from the bad effects of the sun

Pp

pad /pæd/ *n* a thick piece of soft material used to protect or clean a part of your body or a wound

paper /'peɪpə/ *n* **1** thin material used for writing, drawing or printing on **2** a newspaper

parachuting /'pærəʃuːtɪŋ/ *n* a sport or activity using a parachute

park /pɑːk/ *n* a large area with trees and grass in a town where you can walk or play games

passionate /'pæʃənət/ *adj* with very strong, deep feelings: *She is passionate about caring for animals.*

plain /'pleɪn/ *n* a large area of flat land

plane /'pleɪn/ *n* **1** a vehicle with wings and an engine which can fly **2** a tool used for making wooden surfaces smooth

planet /'plænɪt/ *adj* one of the large masses like the Earth, which go around a sun

plastic /'plæstɪk/ *adj* a strong man-made material used for strong containers, toys etc.: *If you drop a plastic bowl, it will not break.*

poison /'pɔɪzən/ *n* (no pl) a substance that kills or harms you if it gets into your body

poisonous /'pɔɪzənəs/ *adj*: *a poisonous snake*

pollute /pə'luːt/ *v* to make the air, water, ground or dirty and dangerous for people, animals and plants: *Nearby factories are polluting the air and water of the town.*

pollution /pəˈluːʃən/ n (no pl): *Pollution of the air, water and earth is destroying our planet.*

poor /pɔː/ adj **1** not having very much money: *She was too poor to buy clothes for her children.* **2** needing kindness or help: *The poor animal hadn't been fed.* **3** not of a good standard: *This work is very poor.*

port /pɔːt/ n a place where boats are safe

possibility /ˈpɒsɪbɪlɪti/ n something that may happen or may be true: *There's a possibility of losing our jobs.*

possible /ˈpɒsɪbəl/ adj **1** it can be done **2** it may happen or it may be true but it is not certain adv **possibly**

power /ˈpaʊə/ n **1** strength or force: *Electricity is a type of power.* **2** control over people and places: *The president has a lot of power.*

power station /ˈpaʊə ˌsteɪʃən/ n a place where electricity is produced

practical /ˈpræktɪkəl/ adj **1** relating to real situations not ideas **2** sensible and good at dealing with problems **3** designed to be useful not attractive: *You need practical shoes for a walking holiday.* **4** good at repairing or making things with your hands

predict /prɪˈdɪkt/ v to say what is going to happen in the future: *The teacher predicted that we all would pass the examination.*

prediction /prɪˈdɪkʃən/ n a statement that something is going to happen in the future: *Your prediction about the weather was wrong.*

press /pres/ n (no pl) all newspapers, magazines and reporters working for them: *the freedom of the press*

prevent /prɪˈvent/ v **1** to stop something from happening **2** to stop someone from doing something

produce /prəˈdjuːs/ v **1** to have something as a result: *This drug produced bad side effects.* **2** to make something, especially in large amounts: *This factory produces 500 cars a day.* **3** to grow something: *The farm produces wheat.*

prosperity /prɒˈsperɪti/ n (no pl) richness; having a lot of money, or success or good luck

prosperous /ˈprɒspərəs/ adj rich: *a prosperous family*

protect /prəˈtekt/ v to prevent something or someone from being harmed or damaged: *The fence is to protect the farmer's cattle.*

pub /pʌb/ n a place, usually in Britain or Ireland, where you can buy and drink alcohol, a bar

pull /pʊl/ v to move something towards yourself or by going in front of it: *He pulled his hand out of the hot water. The horse pulled the cart along the road.*

pyramid /ˈpɪrəmɪd/ n **1** an ancient stone building found in Egypt with four triangle - shaped walls which slope towards a point at the top **2** an object that has this shape

Qq

queen /kwiːn/ n the female ruler of a country; the wife of the king

queue /kjuː/ n a line of people or vehicles waiting for something

quick /kwɪk/ adv moving or happening fast adv **quickly**

quiet /ˈkwaɪət/ adj **1** not making a lot of noise: *Please be quiet in the library.* **2** without much activity: *The shops are quiet during the week.*

Rr

racket /ˈrækɪt/ n the object used for hitting the ball in tennis

rain forest /ˈreɪnfɒrɪst/ n a forest in areas where there is a lot of rain: *The tropical rainforests are being destroyed.*

rational /ˈræʃənəl/ adj based on real facts or scientific knowledge not feelings adv **rationally**

receive /rɪˈsiːv/ v to get something or be given something: *Did you receive my letter?*

recognise /ˈrekəgnaɪz/ v **1** to know someone or something because you have seen them before **2** to realise that someone or something is good: *Her beautiful singing voice was recognised at an early age.*

record /ˈrekɔːd/ n **1** a round thin flat piece of plastic that stores sounds, and which we play on a machine (a record player) to hear the sounds **2** information that is written down and kept: *The doctor kept a record of all serious diseases in the village.* **3** something done better, quicker, etc. than anyone else has done it: *He holds the world record for high jump.*

recover /rɪˈkʌvə/ v to get better, or get back to the usual state: *She has had a bad illness but she is recovering now.*

recycle /ˌriːˈsaɪkəl/ v to treat something so that you can use it again: *Glass, aluminium, cans and newspapers and magazines can all be recycled.*

recycling plant /ˌriːˈsaɪklɪŋ plɑːnt/ n a place where used goods such as bottles and newspapers go through a process so that they can be used again

reduce /rɪˈdjuːs/ v to make something smaller or less: *They've reduced the prices of computers.*

referee /ˌrefəˈriː/ n a person who watches a game and decides if it is fair

remain /rɪˈmeɪn/ v to stay: *I went to the city but my brother remained at home.*

reserved /rɪˈzɜːvd/ adj shy, not happy to talk about your feelings and thoughts: *He's a very reserved man.*

restaurant /ˈrestərɒnt/ n a place where you can buy and eat a meal

retire /rɪˈtaɪə/ v to stop work because of old age or illness: *He retired from the business when he was 65.*

rhinocerous /raɪˈnɒsərəs/ n a large heavy animal with thick skin and a horn on its nose

ride /raɪd/ v (**rode, ridden, riding**) to sit on and control the movement of a horse or bicycle

right /raɪt/ n (no pl) **1** what is fair and good: *You must learn the difference between right and wrong* **2** what is or should be allowed by law: *We must work for equal rights for everybody* **3** the side opposite to the left side: *The school is on the left of the road and his house is on the right.*

river /ˈrɪvə/ n a continuous flow of water along a course to the sea: *The longest river in Africa is the River Nile.*

roast lamb /ˌrəʊst ˈlæm/ n (no pl) lamb meat which has been cooked by baking it without water

robot /ˈrəʊbɒt/ n a machine controlled by a computer which can do the jobs that humans usually do

rocket /ˈrɒkɪt/ n a thing driven into the air by burning gases, used to lift a weapon or space craft off the ground

role /rəʊl/ n a character in a play or film: *He played the role of the old king in our school play.*

romantic /rəʊˈmæntɪk, rə-/ adj showing strong feelings of love

room /ruːm/ n a part of a building which has walls, floor and ceiling: *The living room is my favourite room in the house.*

roughly /ˈrʌfli/ adv **1** about: *There were roughly thirty people in the room.* **2** not gently

Ss

sail /seɪl/ v **1** to travel on water: *His ship sails today.* **2** to direct a boat with sails n **sailing**

salmon /ˈsæmən/ n a large fish with silver skin and pink flesh

Mini-dictionary

satellite /'sætəlaɪt/ *n* an object sent into space to receive signals from one place in space and send them to another place in space

save /seɪv/ *v* **1** to help someone or something to be safe **2** to keep something, especially money so that you can use it again some other time **3** to use less of something; not to waste it

say /seɪ/ *v* (**said, said, saying**) **1** to speak words **2** to express a thought, feeling or opinion

scared /skeəd/ *adj* afraid, frightened

school /skuːl/ *n* a place where children are taught

science /'saɪəns/ *n* the study of nature and the way things in the world are made, or work: *The chief sciences are chemistry, physics and biology.*

science fiction /,saɪəns 'fɪkʃən/ *n* (no pl) stories about the future or about life on other planets: *I love science fiction films.*

scientific /,saɪən'tɪfɪk/ *adj* about science or completed using the methods of science *adv* **scientifically**

scientist /'saɪəntɪst/ *n* a person who studies or works in science

score /skɔː/ *v* to win points in a game: *United scored two goals.*

scream /skriːm/ *v* to give a loud, high cry: *He screamed with fear.*

sea /siː/ *n* a large area of salty water: *the Dead Sea*

self-defence /,self dɪ'fens/ *adj* something you do to protect yourself

sewage /'sjuːɪdʒ, 'suː-/ *n* waste material from the human body carried away in the sewers: *The city needs a new sewage system.*

shark /ʃɑːk/ *n* a large, dangerous fish with sharp teeth

sharp /ʃɑːp/ *adj* **1** able to see things far away or very small: *sharp eyes* **2** able to cut easily: *a sharp knife*

shop /ʃɒp/ *n* a building or room in a building where you can buy things

short /ʃɔːt/ *adj* **1** not long in distance or length: *She's got short brown hair.* **2** happening for only a little time: *I'm going on a short trip to Thailand.*

shorts /ʃɔːts/ *pl n* trousers which stop above the knee: *a pair of shorts*

sinister /'sɪnɪstə/ *adj* appears to be bad or evil: *There was a sinister look on the monster's face.*

skate /skeɪt/ *n* a special shoe with wheels or a blade under it: *roller skates*

skateboard /'skeɪtbɔːd/ *n* a narrow board with small wheels on which you can ride for fun or sport

skateboarding /'skeɪtbɔːdɪŋ/ *n* the sport of skating on a skateboard

skating /'skeɪtɪŋ/ *n* the sport of moving or dancing on ice or the ground while wearing special shoes

ski /skiː/ *n* a long thin, narrow piece of wood, plastic or metal, used in pairs for travelling on snow

ski /skiː/ *v* to go on skis, especially for sport: *I love skiing. n* **skiing**

skin /skɪn/ *n* the outside of a person, animal, vegetable or fruit: *You can make shoes from the skins of animals.*

skirt /skɜːt/ *n* a piece of clothing for girls and women which fits around the waist and hangs down like a dress.

sleepy /sliːpi/ *adj* **1** tired and ready to sleep: *I always feel sleepy after lunch.* **2** quiet and without much activity: *They live in a sleepy little town near the sea.*

sloth /sləʊθ/ *n* a South American animal which moves very slowly

slow /sləʊ/ *adj* taking a long time; not fast: *a slow journey adv* **slowly**

small /smɔːl/ *adj* little, not big

smash /smæʃ/ *v* to break into small pieces: *She smashed the cup.*

smile /smaɪl/ *v* turning up the corners of your mouth to show you are pleased or happy: *a happy smile*

soft /sɒft/ *adj* **1** moving inward when pressed: *a soft bed* **2** feeling smooth and pleasant

solar /'səʊlə/ *adj* of or using the sun: *solar energy*

solar system /'səʊlə 'sɪstəm/ *n* the sun and all the planets that move around it: *Jupiter is the biggest planet in the solar system.*

space capsule /'speɪs 'kæpsjuːl/ *n* the part of a spaceship in which people live and work

space craft /'speɪs krɑːft/ *n* a vehicle that can travel in space

space station /speɪs steɪʃən/ *n* a large space craft which stays above the Earth as a base for people travelling or working in space: *the Russian space station Mir*

spaceport /'speɪspɔːt/ *n* a port where space craft can land and take off

space probe /'speɪs prəʊb/ *n* a space craft without people in it which is sent into space to collect information about conditions there

space suit /'speɪs suːt, sjuːt/ *n* a special suit to wear in space

special /'speʃəl/ *adj* not ordinary but different in some way and often better than what is usual

spend /spend/ *v* (**spent, spent, spending**) **1** to give out money: *How much money do you spend each week?* **2** to pass or use time: *I spent an hour reading.*

sports centre /'spɔːts 'sentə/ *n* a place where you can do different sports

spring /sprɪŋ/ *n* the season after winter

square /skweə/ *n* a shape with four straight sides of equal length

squash /skwɒʃ/ *n* a game played by two people who hit a small rubber ball against the four walls of a court

star /stɑː/ *n* **1** a small point of light that can be seen in the sky at night **2** a five-pointed shape **3** a famous or very skilful actor/actress, sportsperson or singer: *a film star*

star /stɑː/ *v* (**starred, starred, starring**) to appear as the main actor/actress: *Madonna starred in the film.*

station /steɪʃən/ *n* a building where trains and buses stop so that people can get on and off, or where they begin or end their journey

steam train /'stiːm treɪn/ *n* a train that is operated by steam

stick /stɪk/ *n* **1** a long thin piece of wood: *We made a fire out of dry sticks.* **2** a long, curved piece of wood used for hitting the ball in sports such as hockey

stick insect /'stɪk ,ɪnsekt/ *n* a kind of small insect that looks like a stick

stomach /'stʌmək/ *n* the part of the body into which food goes when it is swallowed

stone /stəʊn/ *n* **1** a small piece of rock **2** rock: *This house is made of stone.*

strange /streɪndʒ/ *adj* (**stranger, strangest**) **1** unusual, surprising and different **2** unusual; not what you are used to: *a strange town*

strict /strɪkt/ *adj* severe, especially about behaviour: *Our teacher is very strict; we have to do what she says.*

strong /strɒŋ/ *adj* **1** someone who is strong is able to lift heavy things and do hard physical work **2** not easily broken or damaged **3** powerful: *He is a strong leader.* **4** a strong taste or smell is one which you notice easily: *strong coffee, a strong smell of gas.*

study /'stʌdi/ *v* (**studied, studied, studying**) to spend time learning about something

success /sək'ses/ *n* **1** (no pl) when you achieve what you've been trying to do: *his success in the exam* **2** (pl **successes**) a thing which succeeds: *Her party was a success; everyone enjoyed it. adj* **successful**

suddenly /ˈsʌdnli/ *adv* happening quickly or when you don't expect it: *I suddenly saw my friend.*

suggest /səˈdʒest/ *v* to say to someone that something is a good idea: *I suggest that it would be quicker to travel by train.*

summer /ˈsʌmə/ *n* the season between spring and autumn when the weather is hottest

sumo wrestling /ˌsuːməʊ ˈreslɪŋ/ *n* a kind of wrestling from Japan

sunlight /ˈsʌnlaɪt/ *n* (no pl) natural light from the sun

superb /sjuːˈpɜːb, suː-/ *adj* very fine: *Her dancing is superb.*

supplies /səˈplaɪz/ *pl n* things you need for your daily life: *We cannot get supplies to the village because of the snow.*

surface /ˈsɜːfəs/ *n* the outside, flat part or top of something: *Don't scratch the surface of the table.*

survive /səˈvaɪv/ *v* to go on living: *The man was very ill but he survived.*

survivor *n*: *There were two survivors from the accident.*

swim /swɪm/ *v* (**swam, swum, swimming**) to move through water using your hands and feet. *n* **swimming** *n* **swimmer** someone who swims.

sword /sɔːd/ *n* a sharp, pointed weapon like a long knife that you hold in your hand and fight with

Tt

table tennis /ˈteɪbəl tenɪs/ *n* ping pong, a game played on a table in which players hit a small ball to each other across a low net

take /teɪk/ *v* (**took, taken, taking**) **1** to move someone or something from one place to another. **2** to carry or have something with you: *Don't forget to take your keys with you!* **3** to steal something: *Someone's taken my wallet!* **4** to go with someone to a place: *They took us to the zoo.* **5** to need a period of time to complete something: *It takes 10 minutes to get to my house from here.*

take off /teɪk ˈɒf/ *v* (used about a plane) to leave the ground

take on /ˌteɪk ˈɒn/ *v* to give a job to

take out /ˌteɪk ˈaʊt/ *v* to remove something: *The dentist took out three of her teeth.*

tall /tɔːl/ *adj* having a greater height than normal: *He's the tallest boy in the class. The Empire State building is very tall.*

talented /ˈtæləntɪd/ *adj* able to do a particular thing very well: *a very talented actor*

taxi /ˈtæksi/ *n* a car with a driver who you pay to drive you somewhere

teach /tiːtʃ/ *v* (**taught, taught, teaching**) **1** to give lessons in a subject at a school or college **2** to show someone how to do something

teacher /ˈtiːtʃə/ *n* someone whose job is to teach

team /tiːm/ *n* a group of people who play games or work together a football team

technology /tekˈnɒlədʒi/ *n* (no pl) using the knowledge we get from science to make things in factories or build things: *new technology in computers*

telepathic /teleˈpæθɪk/ *adj* able to communicate thoughts directly to someone else's mind without speaking or writing

tennis /ˈtenɪs/ *n* (no pl) a game in which two or four players use rackets to hit a ball to each other over a net *n* **tennis player**

terrible /ˈterɪbəl/ *adj* very bad or unpleasant: *The food at the hotel was terrible.*

tie /taɪ/ *n* a narrow band of cloth worn around the neck

thick /θɪk/ *adj* **1** with a large distance between one side and the other **2** difficult to see through: *thick clouds, thick smoke* **3** if a liquid is thick it doesn't flow easily **4** (informal) stupid

thin /θɪn/ *adj* **1** narrow, not thick **2** not having much fat on your body: *You should eat more, you're too thin.*

tiger /ˈtaɪgə/ *n* a large wild cat with yellow and black lines on its fur

tiny /ˈtaɪni/ *adj* (**tinier, tiniest**) very small

tooth /tuːθ/ *n* (pl **teeth**) one of the hard white things in your mouth that you use for biting food

torch /tɔːtʃ/ *n* (pl **torches**) an electric light you can carry around

touch /tʌtʃ/ *v* **1** to put your hand or another part of your body on or against something **2** to bring, put or be on or against something: *The branches of the tree touched the water.*

tournament /ˈtʊənəmənt/ *n* (no pl) a competition in which several teams are playing: *a chess tournament*

traffic jam /ˈtræfɪk ˌdʒæm/ *n* a line of cars and other vehicles which can only move forward very slowly or not at all

train /treɪn/ *v* **1** to study how to do a job **2** to teach someone how to do something **3** to prepare for a sports event by exercising or practising

trainers /ˈtreɪnəz/ *pl n* special shoes for playing sport

training /ˈtreɪnɪŋ/ *n* **1** when someone is taught the skills they need to do something **2** physical exercise that you do to prepare for a sports event: *Training is important to become a good athlete.*

tram /træm/ *n* an electric vehicle for carrying passengers which moves along the street on metal tracks

transport /ˈtrænspɔːt/ *n* a vehicle or system of buses, trains etc which you use to go from one place to another

treat (a disease) /triːt/ *v* to try and cure an illness: *Doctors are trying a new way to treat the disease.*

treatment /ˈtriːtmənt/ *n* a way of making a sick person better: *The doctor's treatment made him better.*

turn into /ˈtɜːn ˈɪntuː/ *v* to change and become a completely different thing or person: *He wants to turn the house into a hotel.*

Uu

umpire /ˈʌmpaɪə/ *n* a person who decides about the points won in a game, especially in cricket and tennis

unconscious /ʌnˈkɒnʃəs/ *adj* not knowing what is happening or feeling anything: *After she hit her head, she was unconscious for a few minutes.*

underground /ˈʌndəgraʊnd/ *n* a railway that goes under the ground: *to travel by underground*

unfortunately /ʌnˈfɔːtʃənətli/ *adv* used to say that you wish something had not happened or was not true: *Unfortunately the picnic was cancelled because of rain.*

uninhabited /ʌnɪnˈhæbɪtɪd/ *adj* where nobody lives: *an uninhabited island*

usually /ˈjuːʒuəli/ *adv* what happens in most situations or on most occasions: *We usually have dinner at 8 o'clock.*

Vv

vampire bat /ˈvæmpaɪə ˈbæt/ *n* a South American bat which lives by sucking the blood of other creatures

Mini-dictionary

vegetable /ˈvedʒtəbəl/ *n* a plant such as a carrot, cabbage or a potato which is grown to be eaten

vehicle /ˈviːɪkəl/ *n* something such as a bicycle, car or bus which carries people, goods or equipment

volleyball /ˈvɒlibɔːl/ *n* a game in which two teams hit a ball to each other across a net with their hands and try not to let it touch the ground

volunteer /ˌvɒlənˈtɪə/ *n* a person who offers to do something: *We want some volunteers to deliver food to old people.*

vote /vəʊt/ *v* to choose with other people someone for an official position, for example by marking a paper with a cross or by putting up your hand at a meeting

vulture /ˈvʌltʃə/ *n* a large bird that eats dead animals

Ww

washing up /ˌwɒʃɪŋ ˈʌp/ *n* the washing of plates, knives and dishes

waste /weɪst/ *n* (no pl) **1** used, damaged or unwanted things **2** a wrong or bad use of something: *The meeting was a waste of time.*

wastepaper basket /ˌweɪstˈpeɪpə ˌbɑːskɪt, ˈweɪstˌpeɪpə-/ *n* a small basket in which you put unwanted things

water skiing /ˈwɔːtə ˌskiːɪŋ/ *n* a sport in which a boat pulls you across water with skis on your feet

weapon /ˈwepən/ *n* a thing with which you fight: *A gun is a weapon.*

weigh /weɪ/ *v* to have a particular weight: *The fish weighed two kilos.*

weight /weɪt/ *n* the heaviness of something

well /wel/ *adv* (see **good**)

werewolf /ˈweəwʊlf, ˈwɪə-/ *n* a person who, in some stories, changes into a wolf

west /west/ *n* the direction towards the place where the sun goes down. *adj* in the west or facing west: *on the west coast of Africa*

whale /weɪl/ *n* a very large animal that looks like a very large fish and lives in the sea

wild /waɪld/ *adj* **1** not trained to live with people **2** living in the natural state: *We picked the wild flowers.*

wildlife /ˈwaɪldlaɪf/ *n* (no pl) animals or plants living in the natural state

windsurfing /ˈwɪndsɜːfɪŋ/ *n* the sport of sailing across water by standing on a special board and holding onto a large sail *n* **windsurfer**

wing /wɪŋ/ *n* a movable part of the body of a bird or insect which it uses to fly

winter /ˈwɪntə/ *n* the season when the weather is coldest between autumn and spring

wise /waɪz/ *adj* (**wiser, wisest**) having or showing good sense and cleverness; able to understand things and make the right decisions: *wise old man*

wizard /ˈwɪzəd/ *n* a man in stories who has magic powers

wolf /wʊlf/ *n* (pl **wolves** /wʊlvz/) a wild animal that looks like a large dog

wonderful /ˈwʌndəfəl/ *adj* very good

wood /wʊd/ *n* **1** a material made from the trunk and branches of trees **2** a small forest

worldwide /ˌwɜːldˈwaɪd/ *adj* everywhere in the world

Yy

yawn /jɔːn/ *v* to open your mouth wide and breathe in because you are tired or do not find something interesting: *I couldn't stop yawning.*

Zz

zero gravity /ˌzɪərəʊ ˈɡrævəti/ *n* (no pl) the absence of gravity

zodiac /ˈzəʊdɪæk/ *n* a diagram showing the position of the planets and the stars at different times, which is used to see how the planets and the stars may influence your character and life: *What sign of the zodiac are you?*

zoo /zuː/ *n* a place where different types of wild animals are kept for people to look at and study

END-OF-YEAR SELF-ASSESSMENT

Grade yourself in the following way:

- [A] I have no problems.
- [B] I sometimes have difficulties.
- [C] I have a lot of problems with this.

Speaking

- ☐ Talking about yourself – personal information, family, hobbies, etc.
- ☐ Telling stories
- ☐ Expressing opinions – saying what you think
- ☐ Using English in the class – asking for things, giving excuses
- ☐ Describing people
- ☐ Describing places
- ☐ Using English outside the class – shops, on the phone, to tourists

Writing

- ☐ a formal letter
- ☐ a tourist brochure
- ☐ a story
- ☐ a biography
- ☐ a school magazine article
- ☐ a horoscope
- ☐ paragraph plans
- ☐ notes

Reading (texts in this book)

- ☐ magazine articles
- ☐ stories
- ☐ information texts, e.g. encyclopedia
- ☐ letters
- ☐ brochures

Listening

- ☐ to your teacher
- ☐ to stories (on the cassette)
- ☐ to dialogues (on the cassette)
- ☐ to radio programmes (on the cassette)

Grammar

- ☐ Comparative and superlative adjectives
- ☐ Plans and intentions
- ☐ Past simple
- ☐ Past continuous
- ☐ Present perfect
- ☐ Present perfect/past simple
- ☐ Questions
- ☐ Question tags
- ☐ Passives
- ☐ Conditional sentences
- ☐ *Used to*
- ☐ Predictions

Now write an 'end of year' report on your English. See if your teacher agrees!

Good luck next year!

Fact or fantasy?
Lesson 19 - Fact
Lesson 20 - Fact

Page 79 b All true.

Irregular verb list

Infinitive	Past simple	Past participle
be	was/were	been
begin	began	begun
bend	bent	bent
bite	bit	bitten
break	broke	broken
bring	brought	brought
build	built	built
buy	bought	bought
catch	caught	caught
choose	chose	chosen
come	came	come
cost	cost	cost
cut	cut	cut
do	did	done
draw	drew	drawn
dream	dreamt/dreamed	dreamt/dreamed
drink	drank	drunk
drive	drove	driven
eat	ate	eaten
fall	fell	fallen
feed	fed	fed
feel	felt	felt
fight	fought	fought
find	found	found
fly	flew	flown
forget	forgot	forgotten
get	got	got
give	gave	given
go	went	gone
grow	grew	grown
have	had	had
hear	heard	heard
hide	hid	hidden
hit	hit	hit
hold	held	held
hurt	hurt	hurt
keep	kept	kept
know	knew	known
lay	laid	laid
learn	learnt/learned	learnt/learned
leave	left	left
lose	lost	lost
make	made	made
mean	meant	meant
meet	met	met
pay	paid	paid
put	put	put
read	read	read
ride	rode	ridden
ring	rang	rung
run	ran	run
say	said	said
see	saw	seen
sell	sold	sold
send	sent	sent

Infinitive	Past simple	Past participle
shine	shone	shone
shoot	shot	shot
show	showed	shown/showed
sing	sang	sung
sink	sank	sunk
sit	sat	sat
sleep	slept	slept
speak	spoke	spoken
spell	spelt	spelt
spend	spent	spent
stand	stood	stood
steal	stole	stolen
stick	stuck	stuck
swim	swam	swum
take	took	taken
teach	taught	taught
tell	told	told
think	thought	thought
throw	threw	thrown
understand	understood	understood
wake (up)	woke (up)	woken (up)
wear	wore	worn
win	won	won
write	wrote	written

Phonetic chart

CONSONANTS

SYMBOL	KEYWORD
/ p /	pen
/ b /	back
/ t /	tea
/ d /	day
/ k /	key
/ g /	got
/ tʃ /	cheer
/ dʒ /	jump
/ f /	fat
/ v /	video
/ θ /	thing
/ ð /	then
/ s /	soon
/ z /	zoo
/ ʃ /	fish
/ʒ /	pleasure
/ h /	hot
/ m /	come
/ n /	sun
/ ŋ /	sung
/ l /	led
/ r /	red
/ j /	yet
/ w /	wet

VOWELS

SYMBOL	KEYWORD
/ iː /	sheep
/ ɪ /	ship
/ e /	bed
/ æ /	bad
/ aː /	calm
/ ɒ /	pot
/ ɔː /	saw
/ ʊ /	put
/ uː /	boot
/ ʌ /	cut
/ ɜː /	bird
/ ə /	ago

DIPHTHONGS

SYMBOL	KEYWORD
/ eɪ /	make
/ əʊ /	note
/ aɪ /	bite
/ aʊ /	now
/ ɔɪ /	boy
/ ɪə /	here
/ eə /	there
/ ʊə /	tour